PETER ALLISS'
GOLF HEROES

This edition published in Great Britain in 2003 by
Virgin Books
Thames Wharf Studios
Rainville Road
London W6 9HA

First published in Great Britain by Virgin Books 2002.
Copyright © Peter Alliss 2002

A catalogue record for the book is available from the British Library.
ISBN 0 7535 0856 7

Designed by Smith & Gilmour
Printed and bound in Italy by L.E.G.O. Spa, Vicenza

PETER ALLISS' GOLF HEROES

PETER ALLISS

Virgin BOOKS

CONTENTS

SEVE BALLESTEROS

Until Seve came along, Arnold Palmer was the most exciting and charismatic golfer I had ever seen. However, with his dark good looks, flashing smile and incredible skills, Seve lifted the game through the 1970s and 1980s. He was fallible, he smashed the ball with all his might, went boldly for flags when they were placed in virtually impossible positions, escaped from monstrous situations, and always there was that dashing smile to captivate all and sundry.

The interesting thing about Ballesteros is that he came from the 'wrong end' of Spain. Golf had boomed on the Costa del Sol in the mid-1960s. The growth of the game there has been quite extraordinary: over the last 40 years golf courses have sprung up like mushrooms in a fertile field. That's not to say that golf was unheard of in the north, though. Seve was born in Pedrena, not a million miles away from Santander, a thriving

26th place in the Order of Merit but remained unnoticed – except by one professional, the mighty Roberto de Vicenzo, who had seen him play on a number of occasions and talked endlessly of this young player and his tremendous promise.

In 1975 the Open Championship was played at Carnoustie. Seve failed to make the final 36 holes, but 1976 saw a definite move in the right direction. He finished well in both the Portuguese and the Spanish Opens, but an early appearance in the PGA Championship at Royal St George's in Kent led to opening rounds of 84 and 78 and, hardly surprisingly, he failed to make the cut. Come the Open in July at Royal Birkdale, though, Seve opened up with a 69, which put him in a tie for the lead with Christy O'Connor Jr and Norio Suzuki of Japan. Although O'Connor's uncle, the fabled Christy Senior, had threatened many times to win the championship, and indeed deserved at least

Seve's contribution to British and European golf will be remembered for ever more.

seaport not far from the French border and the exotic town of Biarritz. Seve's family were involved in the game. His uncle, Ramon Sota, was a player of some note, and in spite of a rather ponderous style had many fighting qualities which his young nephew took on board, honed and improved.

Seve made rapid progress once he got himself a couple of proper golf clubs, and broke 80 for the first time when he was just twelve. Before his seventeenth birthday Seve turned pro, the youngest person ever to do so in Spain. His first tournament as a pro was the Spanish PGA Championship. He was not successful there and was in fact disappointed three times in a row, but then he won the Spanish Under-25 Championship. That year he won over £3,000, and by the time 1975 had ended he had risen to

one victory, neither Christy Junior, Suzuki or Seve were expected to be in serious contention after the second round.

Seve started his second round rather fitfully and dropped several strokes, but on the inward nine he put together a tremendous birdie run for another 69. This put him two strokes ahead of Johnny Miller. Seve was paired with Miller for the rest of the championship, and in the third round he again made a poor start and was two behind by the end of the first nine. He promptly birdied the 10th, then hit one of his now fabled vast hooks off the 11th tee. In truth, he was very fortunate the ball was found. There was a comical scene before his second shot, Ballesteros trying to find out in which direction the green lay, but he played a magical shot, found the green, and was once again level

Above **Kissing the 1984 claret jug (© Popperfoto).**

Right As elegant as ever,
Seve in 1998 (©Empics).

with Miller. He eagled the 17th, and at the end of the third round had maintained the two-stroke advantage over the American.

By now people were taking a huge amount of interest. However, the fairytale ended when Miller struck a last-round 66 to win the Open in great style. Seve made a number of unforced errors but finished well with a birdie at the 14th and another eagle at the 17th. The shot most people remember, though, is the magical chip shot, played with all the cheerful, arrogant abandon of youth, between the two bunkers, over a little hump to the hole side to get his par four at the final hole. It was not the most spectacular shot Seve has ever played, but, as it turned out, he needed to get down in two to tie Jack Nicklaus for second place. Seve had arrived, and Seve knew he had.

He went on to win the Dutch Open, and later the Lancôme in France, where the manner of his victory played a big role in the creation of the legend of Seve. Arnold Palmer held a four-stroke lead and did nothing wrong over the homeward stretch, hitting every green in regulation, but Seve birdied five holes and was home in 31 for a one-shot victory. And then he won the World Cup for Spain in partnership with Manuel Pinero.

Seve was becoming a world star, but not in his home country. The attitude of the Spanish public towards his golfing achievements was virtually non-existent. It rankled Seve, perhaps even to this day. Still, he went from strength to strength, although there were disappointments along the way. He certainly should have won the Masters in 1986 when Jack Nicklaus became the oldest player to win that event. He was virtually home and dry, then dumped his second shot at the 15th in the water in front of the green, and that was that. How much that affected his future play is hard to tell, but after that he was, in many people's eyes, never quite the player he once was.

Seve was feisty by nature and had many a run-in with his fellow competitors, some of whom thought he had more than a modicum of gamesmanship in his personality. He was accused of coughing at inappropriate moments and getting in players' eye lines during putts – always looking to take advantage of the rules. Well, he certainly wasn't alone there. It was his huge desire to be the best that drove him on. He battled with authority, didn't feature in half the number of Ryder Cup

Pages 10 & 11 Seve plays an iron shot at the 1988 Open Championship. He has always been a great crowd puller (© Popperfoto).

Left Approaching his ball on one of Wentworth's greens, June 1982 (© Empics).

Always there was that dashing smile to captivate all and sundry.

Above **Seve chips from the rough of Royal Lytham & St Annes' 10th hole during the 1988 Open Championship (© Popperfoto).**

Pages 14 & 15 **Celebrating with fellow Spaniard Jose Maria Olazabal at the 1991 Ryder Cup (© Popperfoto).**

teams he could have played for, and his record in America was far inferior to a number of other players of modest talent by comparison. If Seve Ballesteros at his peak wasn't the best player in the world, he was certainly the most exciting, and everywhere outside the United States he always started as firm favourite.

He married Carmen and they soon started a family. Carmen was the daughter of one of Spain's leading bankers, and a story is told that her mother was not keen on Carmen marrying someone whom she classed (so it is said) only a step or two above a caddy. The marriage, though, appears to be very strong, and although Seve's game has slumped dramatically in the last years, his skills look almost identical to those of years ago when he was winning everything in sight. His short game is still magical but, unfortunately, from the tee he's never quite sure in which direction the ball is going to fly. It's hard to imagine that in the course of the last year or so, the beginning of a new millennium, out of all the tournaments Seve entered, he didn't qualify for the last day on more than a handful of occasions, yet still he practised hard, the desire so obviously still there. How draining that must have been!

He doesn't really have to keep playing. Although Seve has a reputation for being very careful with his money, it is said his wife has inherited tens of millions of dollars from her family, so there's no danger of not being able to have a decent Sunday

lunch with an appropriate glass of wine in the years ahead.

He was an inspirational Ryder Cup captain in 1997, running about like a mother hen, much to the annoyance of some of his players, but he had a lot to prove. The matches were played at Valderrama in southern Spain, for the first time outside Great Britain. It had to be a success, and it was, but having captained once, he said 'No, thank you very much' to a second stint, although I did notice that he hinted that he may come back if asked in future years.

I wonder what lies ahead. I can't honestly see him taking part in the Senior Tour in the United States in six or seven years' time, but you never know, by then he may have found the secret of hitting the ball straight again. Golf has been enhanced by the presence of Seve Ballesteros, a player of enormous talent and with that special presence given to so few. Perhaps his most extraordinary victory was his last Open at Royal Lytham & St Annes in 1988, when he defeated Nick Price by one stroke. Seve was magnificent, but how sorry many of us felt for Nick Price, who started the day with a two-stroke lead, had a final round of 68 and was beaten by Seve who went round in 65 – quite remarkable, and one of the great last-round confrontations in championship golf. His contribution to British and European golf will be remembered for ever more. How I wish he could have one last hurrah.

BILLY CASPER

FACT FILE

FULL NAME: William Earl Casper, Jr

BORN: 24 June 1931; San Diego, California, USA

TOURNAMENT WINS: 68
USA 51
Europe 1
Other 8
US Senior 8

MAJORS: 3
Masters 1 (1970 after play-off)
US Open 2 (1959; 1966 after play-off)
The Open 0 (4th 1968)
US PGA 0 (2nd 1958; T2nd 1965; 2nd 1971)
  US Senior Open 1 (1983)

US MONEY LIST WINS: 2 1966 & 1968

RYDER CUP RECORD:
Appearances & Team Wins (W) 8 (1961–75/7W);
captain (non-playing) 1979 (1W)
Matches (Won-Lost-Halved) 37 (20–10–7)
Wins (Singles-Foursomes-Fourballs) 20 (6–8–6)

Above **Casper is one of the most under-rated golfers of the last 50 years** (© Phil Sheldon)

Right **On occasion, Billy takes his clubs out from under the stairs to perform in selected tournaments** (© Phil Sheldon).

Casper is possibly one of the most under-rated golfers of the last 50 years. His record of victories, particularly in the United States, is staggering. This was mainly down to the quality of his straight driving – although he tended, rather like Bobby Locke, to draw the ball from right to left on to the fairway – and his fine judgement of distance, allied to a beautiful touch around the greens. Indeed, once on the prepared surface, there was no better putter. It's interesting to watch old films of him and, indeed, many of the other great players of the day and note how wristy they were when putting – entirely taboo today, probably due to the fact that most greens now resemble billiard tables, so it's just a question of smoothly rolling the ball towards the target rather than giving it a crisp smack.

Casper's an interesting character for many reasons, not least of which is the number of children he and his wife Shirley adopted. Having had a family of their own, they decided to adopt less privileged children, particularly from the Far East. I'm pretty sure they got into double figures, which must have put a bit of a strain on the housekeeping money, particularly as one or two business deals Billy was involved with didn't work out as handsomely as he had hoped. Tragedy struck at the end of the 1990s when one of these adopted children was arrested on a number of charges concerning drugs, theft and – the ultimate sin – murder, for which he was given a life sentence, or, in American terminology, 455 years, although I'm not quite sure how one is supposed to serve out that time. Perhaps it's just their rather unique method of saying you ain't coming out again, son!

Although he was such a family man, he didn't have a great reputation for being very sociable. Still, he captained the Ryder Cup team and played in it on eight occasions. He and I had some titanic battles which, come the end of our international careers, resulted in us being just about all square.

The wonderfully refreshing thing about Casper was that he got on with the game, he played at a brisk pace. How he would cope with today's slowness is beyond my comprehension, but no doubt he would. He was a very good tactical player and could keep his nerve under the most trying circumstances. This quality manifested itself to the greatest extent when he won the US Open Championship at the Olympic Club in San Francisco in the mid-1960s. Arnold Palmer was the obvious favourite, umpteen strokes ahead with nine holes to play, but for some inexplicable reason he went to pieces. Some say he was going for all sorts of records, but I'm not sure that was true; he just played some poor shots, got careless, let his mind wander, and ended up tying with Billy Casper. During the play-off, once again Palmer was well in the lead with nine to go, and once again he followed that with some poor shots. Casper was the eventual winner, a wonderful achievement against the American golfing hero of the day and a tremendously biased crowd.

After his marvellous career on the main tour, he turned to the Senior ranks and continued to dominate for a number of years. Now 70 years of age he still, on occasion, takes his clubs out from under the stairs to perform in selected tournaments. By now, it must be said, he's more or less a curiosity for the young people who, I'm sure, can hardly believe when they look at his enormous girth that he was once one of the world's great stars. Billy has always had a weight problem, regularly going from looking like a matinée idol to two-ton Billy from Boston. He used to put himself on exotic diets, including one based on buffalo steaks.

But look at the overall number of tournaments won in the United States, and his major victories, and you'll see why Billy Casper has a rightful place in the pages of this book. One is left to wonder why he didn't travel better and win a good many more international events.

BOB CHARLES

Bob Charles is in this book for a couple of reasons, one of them the fact that he is the only left-handed golfer to date to win a major championship – the Open at Royal Lytham & St Annes in 1963. Charles, now well into his late sixties, still plays amazingly well on the main Senior Tour in the United States. He's one of the Tour's most prolific winners and, apart from a head of white hair, looks pretty much the same as he did 40 years ago. He was always a meticulous man, one of the best-dressed professionals on and off the golf course – the shoes always beautifully cleaned, a knife crease in the trousers, a well-blended yet subtle combination of colours – with a quiet demeanour and a wonderful putting stroke. I've seen many great putters over the years and it's very difficult to pick out the best, but Charles would be right up there at the top of

where IMG were quite brilliant – have contracts with several companies. Of course you only used the relevant equipment according to which country you were in. This was also the case as far as golf bags were concerned. You would have a contract for carrying a Slazenger, a Dunlop, a Wilson, a MacGregor or whatever bag in one country while using another manufacturer's clubs. It sounds complicated but it really wasn't. It was just a brilliant ploy on Mark McCormack's part to earn more money for his clients and ultimately push up his percentages!

Charles was also one of those professionals lucky enough to have a wonderful wife, Verity – a quiet lady, perhaps a little long-suffering as Bob moved through life slowly and gently. One had the feeling that sometimes he'd sit polishing his shoes for an

'I'm an introvert. I take things seriously, particularly my golf. That's my business and the golf course is my office.'

BOB CHARLES

the tree along with Bobby Locke and Billy Casper.

Charles joined Mark McCormack's IMG very early on in his career, and what a good move that was, for no one came close to challenging him as the world's leading left-handed player. Winning the Open Championship opened a huge number of golfing doors for him. Left-handed players had been pretty poorly catered for over the years, but Charles signed up with some of the biggest golf club manufacturers in the world. It's interesting to note that a world star could have his name on a set of clubs that sold in Australia and a different one that sold in the United States, and the same with the UK and Europe, so you could – and this is

hour to make sure the shine was just right when perhaps Verity was longing to go to the local Palais for a quickstep. And if that was out of the question, perhaps a slow foxtrot, or even a hug and shuffle! Somehow I don't think those occasions came along too often! They were, and still are, very much a together couple, though, just nice people, and I'm so glad they have both played a small but significant part in my golfing life.

Bob's position as the world's top left-hander is now being seriously challenged by Canadian Mike Weir and Americans Phil Mickelson and Steve Flesch. I don't think it will be too long before one of them wins one of the world's majors.

Above **Charles pictured just after his 1963 Open Championship win** (© Popperfoto).

Right **Teeing off during the 1969 Open Championship** (© Popperfoto).

HENRY COTTON

Henry Cotton was born in Holmes Chapel in the county of Cheshire in 1907, and throughout his life he played a major role in the development of British professional golf.

Most golf professionals up to the middle part of the twentieth century were connected with the game of golf through their role as caddies. When the game began to flourish in the middle of the nineteenth century, the 'toffs' of the day would notice the skills of some of the young caddies and become their mentor-patrons. Before long, matches with large sums of money at stake were being organised. Thus professional tournaments began, and the great triumvirate of Vardon, Taylor and Braid emerged.

Cotton's background was very different from those that had gone before. He was definitely middle class and had had a public-school education at Alleyn's in Dulwich, south-east London. It was while at this school that he decided he would like to become a golf professional – a very bold step for the son of an iron foundry owner who I'm sure must have felt his son could have had a very pleasant life playing golf as an amateur. His father took him to see J. H. Taylor (one of the great stalwarts of the game) to have the boy's skills assessed. The main thing J.H. appeared to notice was the fierce concentration Cotton was able to apply to each shot, and he told Cotton Senior that he thought the boy had promise.

Cotton was not a natural golfer and had to work hard to develop his swing, but he seemed to enjoy the hundreds of hours of practice he put in. It was even suggested at the time that he practised until his hands bled. I'm not always sure I believe these stories; after all, to try to hit golf balls with blistered hands is very uncomfortable. If you get to the stage where they're bleeding and you still continue, you're certifiable!

In those days there was no such thing as a professional golfer, you had to be a golf professional. The difference? You couldn't be freelance, you had to be attached to a golf club, and Cotton's first job was that of assistant at the Fulwell Golf Club in Middlesex. He wasn't there long, and when he moved it was to the delightful links course at Rye in East Sussex. It was here he had more time to play and practise but, remember, he was still very young. By the age of nineteen he was the full professional at the Langley Park Golf Club – an amazing rate of progress by anybody's standards. He learnt to stock the shop, how to trade and to give lessons, but right from day one he set his stall out differently from the rest of his fellow professionals: Cotton was dedicated and determined. Many people would say, however, that Cotton was far from being the ideal club professional, but he always had very good staff looking after things whenever he was absent.

He made his first appearance in the Open Championship in 1926 with no great success, but the following year he played very well over the first 36 holes at St Andrews and went on to finish eighth. Winning the championship had now become his main aim, but it seemed that whenever Americans visited our shores they won as a matter of course. In the late 1920s Cotton decided to try his luck in the United States. He learnt much, including the value of being able to hit the ball from right to left. He had invested £300 in the trip and came back with his money intact.

The major change in the fortunes of young Henry Cotton, now 24, came in 1931. He, Aubrey Boomer and my father, Percy Alliss, were not included in the Ryder Cup team travelling to America because they were not resident in the UK. (That looks a strange rule now when you consider they were three of the best players of their day but were still excluded.) Father was signed up, for a considerable fee, by the *Express* to send back reports of the golf; Cotton and Boomer went along

Above **Cotton at his London home, aged just 16** (© Popperfoto).

Right **Colour portrait, 1946** (© Popperfoto).

ostensibly to play in a few tournaments, intending to pool their winnings.

Strange things happened during that trip. Boomer fell in love on the voyage across and was hardly ever seen again, and Cotton was plagued with an outbreak of boils, an ailment that's virtually disappeared today. So father was left to plough a lone furrow, which he did very successfully, tying with the great Walter Hagen in the Canadian Open only to be beaten at the thirty-seventh hole in a play-off. What did father do? Well, being an honourable chap, he split his money with the other two, who had contributed nothing. But all was not lost as far as Henry was concerned, for he met Mrs de Moss, a woman older than he and reputedly from the Fray Bentos family, the huge meat canning company based in South America. She took an immediate shine to Henry and virtually monopolised his entire life from then on.

Below 'England's foremost golfer' photographed at his London flat, 1946 (© Popperfoto).

When they arrived home she had lessons for hours upon end. They played in many local pro-am competitions and were a formidable pair. Mr de Moss left the scene, and Toots (as she was affectionately known) and Henry got married. To say she was a plain-looking woman would be an understatement, but she had the most dynamic personality. To her dying day she spoke English with a fractured accent but she had enormous presence and style. She was very jealous of Henry and hardly ever let him out of her sight, but she was there to provide him with the wherewithal to raise his standard of living to the very highest level. To play professional golf you still had to be attached to a golf club, and Henry had some good addresses over the years: Royal Mid Surrey, Ashridge, Temple, which was then owned by his great friend Raymond Oppenheimer of the South African diamond family; and there was Monte Carlo for the winter. At one stage he had half a dozen servants working for him: butler, chauffeur, gardener, maid, etc. Even those players today making millions, with their private jets and platinum credit cards, don't have that many retainers permanently dancing attendance on them.

Cotton was ten years younger than my father but in most things they were contemporaries. During the years we were friends he often told me how he envied my father's simple swing because he had to work so hard at getting one that would function under pressure. He certainly had everything under control in 1934 when he won his first Open Championship. He'd scattered the field with opening rounds of 67 and 65 and kept the momentum going with a third-round 72, and it looked all over as he went out for the final eighteen holes with a nine-shot lead. But Cotton was not well and had been physically sick before the start of that final round – whether brought on by nerves or as a result of his secret vice of stuffing his face full of cream cakes smothered in strawberry jam when no one was looking, no one can know! He played very poorly over the first twelve holes and it looked for a while as if he might throw away the chance of winning his first Open, but he recovered his composure and at the end of the day won by five. It's interesting to note that his score of 79 in that final round is the highest by a winner of the championship since the early 1900s.

Above **Teeing off in May 1953 (© Empics).**

His knighthood was an honour some say was long delayed. It's a great pity they didn't think of doing it when he was in his sixties rather than eighties.

Above **Playing a crisp iron shot from the fairway, August 1954 (© Empics).**

At one stage
he had half a
dozen servants
working for him.

His second Open victory came at Carnoustie in 1937, this one against the full might of the US Ryder Cup team. For once Cotton's long game deserted him, but his chipping and putting, sometimes rather frail, were absolutely first-class. Time and time again he holed difficult putts, all this during some of the most violent rainstorms ever seen on that coastline during championship play.

Cotton was indeed king; he looked and lived the part. He worked abroad, as my father did, spending many winters in Monte Carlo where he ran a golf school overlooking the harbour. The professional was known on the continent as 'Le Professeur', which had a much better ring to it than 'Get the pro out here!'

The war deprived Cotton of five years' competitive play and, although he figured reasonably well in the immediate post-war championships, he had to wait until 1948 (when he was 41) to win his third Open at the magnificent Muirfield Golf Club on the east side of Edinburgh. He was very mindful of his position in the world of golf and turned down a chance to play in the 1949 Ryder Cup team, for no other reason, I'm sure, than that he didn't want to expose himself to a potentially good thrashing at the hands of some young fresh-faced American professional. He limited his appearances, and for his services he charged either a big fee or nothing. It's fair to say he didn't do many things for nothing, but he was known to do just that when the cause was a good one. He also during these years picked up the art of golf course design, and early on established a reputation of being, at best, quirky. Some of his early courses bear testament to that fact.

I liked him, he was special. He spoke French fluently, drank Perrier water (*very* sophisticated) and was fond of silk neckerchiefs, which on Cotton looked very jaunty. He hated the drab winter months in Britain and was always looking for continental sunshine. He was helped in this matter by Charles Forte, now Lord Forte, of the great Trusthouse chain. The family at one time owned or controlled almost a thousand hotels worldwide. It would not be unfair to say that Cotton cultivated Forte, and Forte repaid him handsomely. There was always a suite for him at one of the hotels, and the only thing Henry ever paid for was his meals and wine. Not a bad deal when you think of some of the wonderful London locations of the Forte hotels of yesteryear.

Above **Cotton clutches the 1948 claret jug at Muirfield** (© Popperfoto).

Below right **Signing an autograph or two at the 1958 Dunlop Masters** (©Popperfoto).

Pages 26 & 27 **Cotton chips on to the green on his way to winning the 1934 Open Championship at Royal St George's** (© Popperfoto).

Eventually, an opportunity came along for him to move to Portugal and create a golf course for the Penina Hotel. Doug Sanders and I actually played a televised match there in 1966 when the course was flat, wet and totally uninteresting. And why should it be anything else? For hundreds of years it had been paddyfields. Concrete waterways crisscrossed the course, there wasn't a tree in sight, and one wondered if this would ever be a thing of great beauty. Would it ever, indeed, match the grandeur of the hotel? Well, it didn't take all that long for the trees to grow, and although the course continued to have drainage problems the development took on a special appeal. Apart from an enforced spell in Spain during the Portuguese 'peasants' revolt', Henry remained true to Penina. He loved to play golf, and if he was in the pro shop there when you arrived, he wasn't too proud to sell you a golf ball or a few tees. Somehow I can't imagine Arnold Palmer or Jack Nicklaus ever doing that.

Henry had a faithful caddy called Pacifico – no, not a young, barefoot urchin from the local village, but a wonderfully stubborn donkey. Pacifico had a special saddle made so a set of golf clubs could be hung from either side. He was pretty well trained on the whole but occasionally let the side down by breaking wind with tremendous gusto, or relieving himself by the side of the green.

It was at Penina that his dear wife Toots died. He phoned me up – I do believe it was on a Christmas morning. They'd had a dish of tea and were about to open their presents. Henry had gone to look out of the window through the trees to the 1st fairway when he heard a cry. He rushed back and took his wife in his arms, but she was dead. 'I never got a chance to say goodbye,' he said to me, rather poignantly. He continued there for a number of years with the love and help of his stepdaughter and was awarded a knighthood, but sadly he, too, died before the investiture. It was an honour some say was long delayed, but there's no doubt he had made some enemies along the way and some of the people who make those decisions have very long memories. It's a great pity they didn't think of doing it when he was in his sixties rather than eighties.

Henry Cotton, golfer, innovator, golf course designer and forward thinker, for it was he, along with Gerald Micklem and Laddie Lucas, who thought up the idea of the Golf Foundation. He left many monuments to his life in golf, and the Alliss family are proud and privileged to have been alongside the great man at many of those wonderful moments.

ERNIE ELS

FACT FILE

FULL NAME: Theodore Ernest Els

BORN: 17 October 1969;
Johannesburg, South Africa

TOURNAMENT WINS: 38
USA 11 (12 with co-sanctioned 2002 Open
Championship (British Open)
Europe 11
Other 16

MAJORS: 3
Masters 0 (2nd 2000)
US Open 2 (1994; 1997)
The Open 1 (2002)
US PGA 0 (3rd 1995)

US MONEY LIST WINS: 0
Highest: 3rd 2000

EUROPEAN ORDER OF MERIT WINS: 0
Highest: 3rd 2000; 2002

HIGHEST WORLD RANKING: 1
3 times (total 9 weeks) 1997–98

PRESIDENTS CUP RECORD:
Appearances & Team Wins (W) 3 (1996–2000/1W)
Matches (Won-Lost-Halved) 15 (6–7–2)
Wins (Singles-Foursomes-Fourballs) 6 (2–2–2)

Above **1998 Open Championship,
Royal Birkdale** (© Popperfoto).

Right **Sinking an eagle putt at the
2001 World Cup** (© Popperfoto).

Pages 30 & 31 **Celebrating
a holed bunker shot at Loch
Lomond's 18th hole, July 2000**
(© Empics).

From a very young age Els was special. No one could ever have accused him of being academic, but his various sporting skills were, once he was out of nappies, quite remarkable. Rugby, cricket, hockey, swimming – all were played with consummate ease, but as he moved into his teens he found that the game of golf gave him more overall pleasure. He could, for example, go out and have enormous fun pottering about on his own without having to wait for numerous colleagues to arrive before the game could begin.

Over the last hundred years South Africa has produced many champions in a wide variety of sports. Some put it down to their upbringing. The white population (in the minority) seemed to have a great desire to succeed in sport, and succeed they certainly did, producing a wonderful array of talent. Opportunity and climate also, of course, have a lot to do with success, but you've still got to have the natural desire and will to go forward.

Els was born in 1969. So much was expected

an easy swing many envied. Victories followed, his best effort to date coming in 1994 when he won the US Open Championship at the famous Oakmont Golf Club after an eighteen-hole play-off against American Loren Roberts and Scotsman Colin Montgomerie.

Ernie is a truly international golfer. If all we read is true, then financially speaking he has been well advised and should be set up for life, so playing golf should become easier. But that, in my experience, is not always the case, particularly if you have an inner drive and a desire to play your best all the time and not let yourself, family or country down.

There's no doubt, if he so wishes and remains injury-free (I'm concerned as he seems to have recurring back problems), he could well be one of the dominant figures in the world of golf, certainly for the next seven or eight years. But it's one thing to have the skill, it's another to have the nerve and desire. Ernie certainly has the nerve, but I'm not

He will continue to thrill and frustrate us over the coming years.

from him in the world of professional golf for he had had a glittering end to his teens, but in spite of his abundance of natural skills he didn't immediately take it by storm. He failed twice to get through the qualifying school, and in 1991 played eight times on the Ben Hogan Tour, a subsidiary circuit that helps foster up-and-coming talent. Then, for some reason, in 1992 he won the South African Open, their PGA Championship and their Masters; Gary Player was the only other professional to have won those three titles in one year. Els ended up winning four of the eight tournaments on the South African Tour, then, in 1993, visited our shores to play on the European Tour. He immediately made a good impression. He was a big man with an open face, a ready smile and

totally convinced he has the fanatical desire to be the best in the world. I don't have any problem with that, although I do admire those players that have this focus, sometimes at the cost of everything else. Then again, some have managed to reach the pinnacle of Everest and remain quite stable, personable and even, on rare occasions, likeable!

Els, I'm sure, will continue to thrill and frustrate us over the coming years. When you analyse his record from those early days in 1984 when he won the World Junior Championship, he has crammed in an awful lot. Not quite in the same fashion as Tiger Woods, but then, when you talk of Tiger, you're speaking about one of the rarest animals ever discovered in the world of sport.

NICK FALDO

FACT FILE

FULL NAME: Nicholas Alexander Faldo

BORN: Welwyn Garden City, Hertfordshie, England

TOURNAMENT WINS: 39
USA 6
Europe 27
Other 6

MAJORS: 6
Masters 3
(1989 after play-off; 1990 after play-off; 1996)
US Open 0 (T1st 1988 lost play-off)
The Open 3 (1987; 1990; 1992)
US PGA 0 (T2nd 1992)

US MONEY LIST WINS: 0
Highest: 12th 1996

EUROPEAN ORDER OF MERIT WINS: 2
1983; 1992

HIGHEST WORLD RANKING: 1
4 times (total 97 weeks) 1990–94

RYDER CUP RECORD:
Appearances & Team Wins (W) 11 (1977–97/4W)
Matches (Won-Lost-Halved) 46 (23–19–4)
Wins (Singles-Foursomes-Fourballs) 23 (6–10–7)

Above **I shall always have the greatest admiration for the way he went about his golfing career** (© Popperfoto).

Right **The 1990 Open Championship winner** (© Popperfoto).

Nick Faldo came rather late to the game of golf. Born in 1957, he was an only child and, like so many, a loner, enjoying cycling and swimming, both very individualistic pastimes. It's been well documented that while in his mid-teens he found himself watching play from the Masters at Augusta National Golf Course on BBC television. Jack Nicklaus caught his eye, and in that split-second Faldo was hooked on the game.

The Faldo family lived in Welwyn Garden City, and as soon as young Faldo let his interest in the game of golf be known his parents got him some clubs and booked him a course of lessons at a local golf club, where the professional was Ian Connelly – someone, incidentally, who got very little acknowledgement from Faldo in later years (I often wondered why). Nick was tall and slim and soon developed a wide rhythmical swing generating tremendous power. He made rapid progress, and it wouldn't be wrong to say he became obsessed with the game. His parents, although comfortably off, were not wealthy and could not indulge their son in his every whim, but they were very supportive and he returned that support by giving the game his total concentration and effort.

He played amateur golf for a few years and as a Youth International in 1974 and 1975 won several important events, including the English Amateur title just a few days after his eighteenth birthday. He turned pro in 1976 and immediately made an impact. He began to put some incredible scores together, but had not yet found any consistency. After winning a couple of tournaments he secured a place in the 1977 Ryder Cup team for Royal Lytham and St Annes. He played well, beating Tom Watson in their singles match.

For whatever reason – and I find this fascinating – he then decided he should be doing better and teamed up with a relatively unknown golf professional by the name of David Leadbetter, who

had turned to teaching for a living. Leadbetter had some rather revolutionary ideas which appealed to Faldo, and soon their partnership grew into a friendship, although that was to sour in later years. Together they dismantled Faldo's swing and started again, although certain traits remain to this day. I'm sure the main change was in the mental approach and physical dedication, the art of finding a way of hitting the ball straight and true when under immense pressure.

The results of this makeover were quite extraordinary: Nick Faldo went on between 1987 and 1996 to win three US Masters and three Open Championship titles. Some of those victories were very hard-fought indeed. However, he rarely threatened to win the US Open or, particularly, the US PGA, which is hard to explain. Why? Well, the United States Golf Association has a reputation for making golf courses very difficult, narrowing the fairways, growing punishing rough, getting the greens lightning fast and then putting the flags in almost ridiculous situations. Occasionally their course set-ups have been severely criticised, and with good reason. Then again, Sandy Tatum, past president and long-time father figure of the United States Golf Association, came up with a very good line when asked if the USGA wanted to embarrass the best golfers in the world: 'We're not trying to embarrass anyone, we're just trying to identify them.' A smart reply, but then Tatum was a very respected San Franciscan lawyer who spent a couple of years at Oxford in the late 1940s and was perhaps the original Yank of that ilk! You would have thought Faldo would have been in his element under such conditions, but it wasn't so.

The British Open and US Masters are two entirely different examination papers. The Masters is played at the same venue every year, and although they tweak it here and there it remains basically the same, whereas the Open Championship moves round seven or eight

locations and players are never quite sure what to expect, although the installation of fairway watering has taken some of the idiosyncrasies out of links golf, where it was not uncommon years ago to see a drive run no more than 100 yards.

But why Faldo should have been so successful at those two events and only rarely figure in the other two has neither rhyme nor reason. For a relatively short period he played wonderfully controlled golf, but somehow a certain 'sparkle' left his game. When he had his wide willowy swing he put some extraordinarily low rounds together and putted like a demon. Once his game was reassembled, he became straight and true, lost quite a bit of distance off the tee and never recaptured that wonderful putting stroke. But his game was such that when the going got tough, he was tough enough to get going.

I don't know whether Faldo quite qualifies for the title 'Enigma' – perhaps only with a small 'e'. He is enormously generous with both his time and his money for a number of causes, mostly to do with young people, yet even after all the exposure he's had he never appears at ease when interviewed.

His interviews today are just as stinted as they were twenty years ago. For whatever reason he hasn't appeared to try, or to bother, to learn the art of communication and work out a technique whereby he can look relaxed in front of camera and 'give' something to the interviewer. His press-room appearances, even when he's had spectacular success, have always been hard work. A pity, because this has led to a lot of misunderstandings, none of which have been eased by the fact that he's been married three times, for which he has taken his share of the blame. Although all the divorces had a touch of acrimony about them, they might have been a great deal worse, and he appears to have come through relatively unscathed. One hopes the children feel the same way.

He doesn't seem to have a great facility for dealing easily with people, particularly those who have worked for or with him. For many years he was with Mark McCormack's mighty IMG organisation, personally looked after by one of the best negotiators around, John Simpson. Then Faldo left the IMG fold, Simpson went some time later, and they set up an office together in

Below **Faldo reflects on another missed cut, this time at Augusta, April 2001** (© Popperfoto).

Right **Chipping on to the green at St Andrews' road hole, July 2000** (© Popperfoto).

'I'm just playing for the love of the game. And for the little cups.'
NICK FALDO

'I hope in ten years' time I'm out of touch with golf altogether, sitting on my tropical beach. Or at least knocking it round for an absolute laugh.'

NICK FALDO

Wimbledon, much to the chagrin of Mark McCormack. But Faldo at this stage was past his best and living on former glories. Suddenly he and Simpson 'divorced' and Faldo moved back under the wing of IMG. McCormack must be a forgiving soul, or perhaps he saw an opportunity to rekindle Faldo's fame in other directions.

When his game started to deteriorate in the late 1990s he decided that David Leadbetter would have to go. Stories of how he broached that news to Leadbetter are many and varied, but it would appear it happened rather in the way musician Phil Collins divorced his wife: Collins simply sent a fax stating 'Marriage Over'. Although he didn't make much of it at the time, I'm sure Leadbetter's bottom lip trembled when he got the fateful news. Round about this time Faldo decided to get himself a new caddy, too, so the trusty Fanny Sunesson – that masterful woman with the

Above **Faldo plays delicately from a bunker at Royal Troon's 1989 Open Championship (© Popperfoto).**

Left **Lining up a putt at the 1982 Suntory World Match Play Championship at Wentworth (© Empics).**

Pages 38 & 39 **Teeing off into the sun at Sandwich during the 1993 British Open, where he finished second to Greg Norman (© Popperfoto).**

commanding voice ('Stand still please, no cameras!') – had to go. This parting also happened under strange circumstances. It was reported that Faldo had bought Fanny a four-wheel-drive off-road vehicle (posh name for a Jeep); they were going to have a bit of lunch and talk of the future. But, no, the parting was swift. I don't know whether it happened before or after lunch, but happen it did. Fanny went off to America and started caddying for, among others, Fred Funk. (Fanny and Funk – what a combination!) Things jogged on, but suddenly Faldo and Fanny were back together on the fairways of the world, and how nice it looked. There are a few signs of revival on Faldo's part.

For all his aloofness, if that's the right word, Faldo is without question the most formidable British golfer of the last 60 years. I'm only sorry he went through a period when he didn't have the warmth of the golfing general public behind him.

The difficulties of his personality created barriers that people couldn't breach, in a similar way to Ben Hogan 40 years earlier. There was a time when I was supposed to have had a feud with Faldo, but it was nothing of the sort. Casual remarks made by both of us were picked up by various journalists, embellished, exaggerated and pursued. Neither of us has ever been a guest in the other's house, and I don't expect either of us ever will be, but I shall always have the greatest admiration for the way Nick Faldo went about his golfing career. I didn't always understand his methods, but for a number of years he made it work brilliantly and gave British golf and golfers something to cheer about.

It wouldn't surprise me if in 2007 when he reaches 50 he decides to pursue another career on the US Senior Tour. If he maintains his health and desire, I'm sure he could be a giant again in the game of golf. Then again, perhaps once is enough.

WALTER HAGEN

FACT FILE

FULL NAME: Walter Charles Hagen

BORN/DIED:
b 21 December 1892;Rochester, New York, USA
d 5 October 1969; Traverse City, Michigan, USA

TOURNAMENT WINS: 67
USA 40
Europe 6
Other 21

MAJORS: 11
Masters 0 (T11th 1936)
US Open 2 (1914; 1919 after play-off)
The Open 4 (1922; 1924; 1928; 1929)
US PGA 5 (1921; 1924; 1925; 1926; 1927)

RYDER CUP RECORD:
Appearances & Team Wins (W) 5
(1927–35/4W – playing captain in all 5);
captain (non-playing) 1937 (1W)
Matches (Won-Lost-Halved) 9 (7–1–1)
Wins (Singles-Foursomes) 7 (3–4)

Above **He was elegant, had
great charm, and large crowds
gathered wherever he played**
(© Popperfoto).

Right **Hagen with the third of
his claret jugs, Sandwich, 1928**
(© Popperfoto).

With his skill and flamboyant lifestyle, Hagen helped change the face of professional golf. He was a great champion, too: to this day only Jack Nicklaus has managed to beat his record of eleven major titles as a professional.

Hagen was one of five children born to William and Louise Hagen, who were both of German extraction. He got into the game of golf at the age of eight caddying for ten cents an hour at a golf club near his home. At a very early age he discovered the art of putting, controlling the stroke with the last two fingers of his left hand (must try that!). His parents did nothing to encourage him in this direction; I expect they thought there was no way he could make a living out of it, for the game in the early years of the twentieth century was virtually unknown in the United States. Little did they know how fast golf would grow, how one day their son would make a fortune playing it. And why should they have known? After all, Walter Hagen was the first one to do so.

His father was a blacksmith working in a car body shop, but Walter was to learn quickly that there was more money in golf. At the age of fourteen he was taken on as an assistant professional at a golf club near Rochester, New York. By the time he was nineteen he had been appointed the professional for the grand sum of $1,200 for an eight-month season. His father joined him on the greenkeeping staff. Perhaps his blacksmith's skills came in handy for repairing some of the new-fangled machines that were coming on to the market. The strange thing was, his father didn't watch his son play a competitive round until 1931, when Walter was nearly 40. His mother never did.

While a young man Hagen wasn't totally convinced that golf was the game for him. He was good at baseball and was offered a trial with the famous Philadelphia Phillys, but after much

thought he turned it down because he thought golf was a game for individuals and that's where he should be, not having to rely on team-mates for success. He learnt the game simply by playing and watching others better than he. Years later, he was amazed how much practice his successors put into the game. Once, while watching Byron Nelson going through a strenuous practice session, he remarked, 'What a shame to waste all those good shots. That's nothing but corporal punishment.' It was said with such intensity; he obviously felt it could ruin one's confidence. If you started to mishit shots, it might be too easy to discover what was going wrong instead of right!

So, with little practice and no teacher, Hagen developed his swing. He had a wide stance and a bit of a sway – his detractors said it was an awful lurch – but everything was correct when the club head met the ball. Most importantly of all, he had good rhythm and balance, although sometimes he used to fall away at the end of the follow-through. He was never afraid of or put off by a bad shot. In fact, he allowed himself four or five poor shots a round, although he considered it a cardinal sin to hit two in a row. He also had the ability to hole a crucial putt when all looked lost. He was elegant, had great charm, and large crowds gathered wherever he played.

In 1920 Hagen crossed the Atlantic to compete in the first post-Great War British Open Championship, played at the Royal Cinque Ports Golf Club near Deal in Kent. He brought with him a number of colour-coordinated golfing outfits and his by now famous black and white shoes, having decided early on that snappy dressing was part of the professional's ensemble. When you see competitors playing today in a very casual style, it's hard to believe that Hagen's wardrobe included dozens of silk shirts, white flannels, red bandanas and a number of white buckskin shoes. For his first championship he also hired an Austro-Daimler

Above **Greeting Bobby Jones at St Andrews. How dapper they both look!** (© Phil Sheldon).

limousine and a butler, but the secretary refused to let him into the clubhouse, saying, 'You can change your shoes in the pros' shop.' After all, the fellow was a professional. Hagen relished the situation, and his behaviour during the championship must have embarrassed the secretary. If he wasn't allowed into the clubhouse there was surely no embargo on the car park. The professionals of the day didn't own motor cars, so Hagen made sure his limousine was parked right in front of the clubhouse, and daily his butler served him lunch with, of course, appropriate wines. The members didn't like it one little bit.

His play during this championship, however, was not great, and he finished last but one of the 54 qualifiers, a fact which in no way dented his ego. The winner, George Duncan, had started poorly, but his last two rounds of 71 and 72 were quite remarkable given the conditions. Hagen's final two rounds were 78 and 85, his aggregate some 26 strokes behind the winner. He fared a lot better the following week when he won the French Open Championship at La Boulie, just outside Paris, and decided he liked Britain and Europe and would surely return. He put his poor play at Deal down to his inability to play a low pitch and run. He was very good at the high pitch, but they tended to be blown away in the wind, and he vowed it would be very different when he came over on his next trip.

And so it was. In 1921, at St Andrews, Hagen broke 80 in every round, and in the morning's play on the final day registered one of the lowest rounds that year, a 72, which put him a stroke ahead of Jock Hutchison and level with the amateur Roger Wethered, the two players who were to tie for the championship later that day. Hagen's final round was a 77, but, as he said at the time, he had nearly got the hang of links golf, and that desirable skill would manifest itself over the next three years.

In 1922, at Royal St George's, Sandwich, the course next to Deal, he became the first American player to win the Open Championship. The scoring was high, and with good reason: the wind blew hard and the rough was formidable. Hagen came from behind with one of the lowest rounds of the championship, a 72, although he was nearly pipped at the post by George Duncan, who took three from the edge of the final green to miss a play-off. At the presentation Hagen looked at his cheque and was not impressed. He thought there should be a few more noughts on the end, so he handed it straight to his caddie with a hearty vote of thanks.

It continued to annoy Hagen that professionals were not allowed into many clubhouses in Britain. It was all very different back in the United States. In the 1923 Open Championship he was runner-up to Englishman Arthur Havers. The committee, being very broadminded, decided to hold the presentation inside the clubhouse and invited Hagen to attend. He didn't accept, making a short speech to the crowd instead and inviting them all to join him for a drink at the local pub. It was clear to all that Hagen was very much his own man.

His appearances in Britain, however, became fewer and fewer, though he returned in 1928 and 1929 and won both Open Championships. The strange thing was, just before the 1928 event he was thrashed in an exhibition match by Archie Compston who finished eighteen up with seventeen to play over 72 holes. It was an unbelievable win. Some said that when Hagen realised he was going to be beaten he thought it a good idea to let the margin be huge, thereby making even bigger headlines. Any publicity was good publicity, after all. Compston, one of the best players of the day, was expected to win the championship and he played very well, but only well enough to finish three strokes behind Walter.

Hagen had married Margaret Johnson in 1917, a lively soul who enjoyed being with a celebrity, which suited Hagen very well. Within a year their only child was born, Walter Jr, but sadly the marriage didn't last. Hagen was just not cut out for married life; he liked to travel and give or attend parties. He didn't really own a home until he retired, but remember, times were very different then. Today's stars jet around the world from one tournament to another, then fly home or on to another venue. Hagen was often away for months on end giving exhibition matches and taking the gate money away in an old suitcase. And what should one do then? Why, spend it, of course.

He was very cavalier in his approach to many things, including golf, and would 'go for broke'

Right **Handing back the Ryder Cup to the PGA at London's Paddington Station, April 1929** (© Popperfoto).

whenever the opportunity arose. It was Hagen who first uttered the immortal words that nobody ever remembered the man who finished second. There wasn't a tremendous number of tournaments to be played in those days, and professionals at this level went 'on the road' playing exhibition matches hither and thither and taking the gate. This could prove very lucrative as golf was growing in popularity at a huge rate of knots. Hagen was an accomplished self-publicist who managed to create an aura about him of a high-living playboy, a drinker, a smoker and a flirt bordering on womaniser. There are many tales of him arriving late and walking on to the 1st tee in full evening dress and the like, but most are either exaggerated or apocryphal. This flamboyant lifestyle and colourful play paid off, though, and changed the face of the game at the same time. Other professionals could see an opportunity to better their lifestyles, upping their fees from a dollar a lesson to two, putting on smarter clothes and generally moving into a higher echelon of society.

In 1930, tiptoeing towards his forties, he set out on a world tour with Joe Kirkwood, the greatest trick-shot artist of the day. They went to Australia, New Zealand, Japan and many other ports of call where the game of golf was played. Hagen loved to travel, loved to see new places. He went big-game hunting in Africa; to Ceylon and India, where he went on shooting expeditions with the Raja of Calcutta; through Malaya and Hong Kong; even into China. His fee for an exhibition match after winning his first US Open Championship was $75, but it rose to $300 soon after the First World War. Not bad, but you can see why Walter preferred to take the gate money.

In 1931 my father, Percy, tied with Hagen after 72 holes for the Canadian Open Championship. They ended level once again after a 36-hole play-off, so off they went into sudden death, Hagen holing a good putt on the first hole to secure the win. My father, in all modesty, thought he should have won, but he missed putt after putt between eight and twelve feet, so much so that at the end of the game Hagen gave him one of his favourite putters and said, 'Here, that could help your putting blues.' It worked for a while, but, like so many other putters belonging to the Alliss family, it finally betrayed him, although I still have that club in my collection.

Hagen's last hurrah came in 1933 when he was a
few years past his best. For a while old memories
came flooding back with rounds of 68 and 72 to
lead the field, but he faded and finished well down
the list. It was the end of an era. The British Open
had always been Hagen's favourite. He used to say,
'If I can have that one, the others can have all the
rest.' Remember that at this time the Masters had
not yet burst on to the golfing scene, yet Hagen has
won more major professional championships
than anyone else in the history of the game, with
the exception of Nicklaus.

Despite his greatness, Hagen saw the game
simply, as a means of earning money to enjoy a
certain lifestyle. 'Twas he who said, 'I never wanted
to be a millionaire, I just wanted to live like one.' It

is said of the mighty Sam Snead that he made a
million and saved two; of Hagen that he made a
million and spent three. He was relaxed and fully
at home with people from all levels of society, and
would invite spectators and the rich and famous
alike along to the pub for a drink. He once kept
President Harding, a keen golfer himself, waiting
while he had a shave, and playing golf with royalty
didn't fill him with awe either. Once, when out
with the Prince of Wales, later the Duke of
Windsor, he said in a loud voice, 'Hey, Eddie, hold
the flag while I putt, will you?'

The game of golf owes a huge debt to Walter
Hagen, a supreme golfer and certainly one of the first
choices for an evening's companion. Sadly, in many
ways those days have long gone – never to return.

BEN HOGAN

FACT FILE

FULL NAME: Benjamin William Hogan

BORN/DIED:
b 13 August 1912; Dublin, Texas, USA
d 25 July 1997; Fort Worth, Texas, USA

TOURNAMENT WINS: 64
USA 63
Europe 1

MAJORS: 9
Masters 2 (1951; 1953)
US Open 4 (1948; 1950 after play-off; 1951; 1953)
The Open 1 (1953)
US PGA 2 (1946; 1948)

US MONEY LIST WINS: 4
1940; 1941; 1942; 1948

RYDER CUP RECORD:
Appearances & Team Wins (W) 2
(1947–51/2W – playing captain 1947/1W);
captain (non-playing) 1949, 1967 (2W)
Matches (Won-Lost-Halved) 3 (3–0–0)
Wins (Singles-Foursomes) 3 (1–2)

Above **September 1949, as non-playing captain, before that year's Ryder Cup** (© Popperfoto).

Right **Winner of his one and only Open Championship, at Carnoustie in 1953** (© Popperfoto).

The third child and second son of Clara and Chester Hogan – like Walter Hagen's father a blacksmith and car mechanic – William Benjamin Hogan was born in 1912 in the town of Dublin, Texas. As the Hogans' first child was christened Royal and the second Princess, you might say the third was lucky to be so-called. In 1921, Hogan Senior found his trade in a slump and left to see if prospects were any better in Fort Worth. The answer was: just a little. Back he went to Dublin to give Clara the news. She told him she wasn't ready to move, certainly not until the children had come to the end of the school term. She wanted to make sure they received a full education. Chester thought this over for a while, then went to his suitcase, took out a revolver and shot himself in the head. He died a day later. At the time Royal was thirteen and Ben nine. Royal worked at three jobs to keep the family solvent and Ben sold newspapers. The suicide of their father left tremendous scars, and the children learnt at a very early age that the mind sometimes leads us to do strange things.

Ben was already into golf, caddying at the nearby Glen Garden Club. He also used to knock golf balls about as he delivered newspapers. He was a true young fanatic, but, in all truth, wasn't very good. However, he kept going for years and was perhaps the most persistent non-achiever of any of the great players that were to follow. He tried everything, even for a time going cross-handed, possibly because he was a natural left-hander, but that soon went by the wayside and he changed to a conventional right-handed grip.

There was another boy who lived close by named Byron Nelson. Little did they know in those early days what tremendous rivalry would come to exist between them. There were some wonderful boyhood duels, Nelson invariably coming out on top, but Hogan's greater persistence helped him win greater fame and a higher reputation than Nelson who, like Bobby Jones, retired early, at the age of 33.

In 1931, when he was nineteen, Hogan set out to play a few tournaments in California with $75 in his pocket to cover expenses. That soon disappeared, and he had to return home. The same thing happened the following year. Hogan didn't have the security of being a club professional, so he would take on odd jobs outside golf. Then off he'd go and blow it all on just a few tournaments. During those years he worked in an oilfield and as a garage mechanic, bank teller, petrol pump salesman, waiter and even a croupier. My bet is that the last of these might have suited his personality the best. Those steely eyes – what a poker player he would have made!

Like many other great golfers, Ben Hogan was blessed with a superb wife, Valerie, who encouraged him in the early part of his career when life was hard and success seemed a million miles away. They drove from tournament to tournament, and on some occasions their diet consisted of oranges and only oranges, but all that hard work finally paid dividends.

Hogan is rated by many as the best striker of the golf ball the world has ever seen, and the supreme strategist. He came only once to play in our Open Championship, at Carnoustie in 1953, and he won. This was my third Open, and I remember the great crowds that appeared hoping to get a glimpse of 'the wee ice man'. He was recovering from a horrendous car accident at the time; just getting himself physically ready to go to the golf course each day took a tremendous effort. In those days the crowds were allowed to roam the fairways, and getting through them and on to the next tee, and then through them again to play your second shot, back on to the green and then on to the next tee took considerable stamina, but Hogan was more than up to the task, improving his score with each of his rounds.

Above **Receiving the Ryder Cup
from Lord Wardington of Alnmouth,
September 1949 (© Popperfoto).**

Right **Another clean Hogan
connection, this time at the
1956 Canada Cup at Wentworth
(© Popperfoto).**

It's worth noting that Hogan was fast
approaching middle age when he first won a
major title: the year was 1946, Hogan was 34. His
tally of victories over the next few years, though,
makes sensational reading. I had the privilege of
watching him play at close hand on a number of
occasions, and at other times, such as in 1967 when
the Ryder Cup was played at the Champions Club
in Houston, Texas, and Hogan was their non-
playing captain. He had an aura about him, and
was a complex man. I'm told by a number of his
acquaintances (he had very few friends) that he
was conscious of the fact that he had had what he
considered no 'formal' education and was always
mindful of 'doing the right thing'. However, he did
not suffer fools at all and was not afraid to put
anyone in their place. During one practice round,

Arnold Palmer, who was then in his pomp,
asked Hogan who he was going to be playing
with in the foursomes the next day. Hogan replied,
with a steely glint in his eye, 'I'm not sure whether
I'm going to pick you yet,' which deflated Arnold
slightly, but he soon perked up, took off in his
newly acquired aeroplane and dive-bombed
the course, in contravention of the rules and
regulations of aviation and to the annoyance
of Hogan. But he got away with it.

One of the most famous sights in golf is the
Swilken Bridge just in front of the 18th tee at St
Andrews. It's said that every player of any note has
at some time or another walked over that bridge
except for Ben Hogan, who visited Scotland just
once to play that championship at Carnoustie. But
rumour has it that he actually stopped off at St

Hogan's house on the outskirts of Fort Worth had just one bedroom. This prompted his great friend Jimmy Demaret to remark, 'I guess Ben doesn't like people to stay over.'

Andrews, perhaps on his way back to get a train from Edinburgh, to look at the Old Course and, indeed, stood on that wondrous old bridge. I'd like to think that happened, but there are so many wonderful tales, many of them apocryphal, about the 'goings-on' at St Andrews over the centuries. But that bridge fascinates me. It's less than four feet wide and it's only a few feet above the water table, so how it could ever have been written up as one of the main links between St Andrews and Cupar is beyond my comprehension. I'm sure there was never a time when the Swilken Burn was a raging torrent bordered by 100ft cliffs and there was only room for a man on horseback, or someone leading a packhorse, to walk over the bridge in single file. So, you see, stories sometimes do stretch the imagination. And why not? There's no one here to argue against it today, and I still would like to think that Hogan, for all his blinkered desire, might have taken a little time

to make a detour and look at the Old Course and the town of St Andrews – and, perhaps, walk over the Swilken Bridge.

I think it's a pity he has left no great legacy of 'golfing secrets'. He wrote a very successful instructional book with the most wonderful illustrations but was very mean with his knowledge – a great pity. There's hardly anything of him on film, at play or in interview. He was quietly elegant, favouring shades of grey, cashmere sweaters, beautifully cut trousers and handmade shoes, but like many others he eventually got the twitch with the putter. He was too proud to try any method that might have helped, he just didn't feel that was right. He persevered, trying to do it the 'right way', but in the end succumbed, even though he could still strike the ball beautifully. It was a privilege to see Hogan at his best. He really was a master of ball striking and strategy. Nobody did it better.

TONY JACKLIN

FACT FILE

FULL NAME: Anthony Jacklin, CBE

BORN: 7 July 1944;
Scunthorpe, Lincolnshire, England

TOURNAMENT WINS: 26
USA 3
Europe 14
Other 7
US Seniors 2

MAJORS: 2
Masters 0 (T12th 1970)
US Open 1 (1970)
The Open 1 (1969)
US PGA 0 (T25th 1969)

US MONEY LIST WINS: 0
Highest: 20th 1970

EUROPEAN ORDER OF MERIT WINS: 0
Highest: 5th 1966

RYDER CUP RECORD:
Appearances & Team Wins (W) 7 (1967–79/0W);
captain (non-playing) 1983, 1985 (W),
1987 (W), 1989 (tied)
Matches (Won-Lost-Halved) 35 (13–14–8)
Wins (Singles-Foursomes-Fourballs) 13 (2–8–3)

Max Faulkner won the Open Championship at Royal Portrush in 1951, but British golf had to wait almost twenty years for a repeat performance. It came at Royal Lytham & St Annes in 1969. Tony Jacklin, who had been promising much for two or three years, suddenly struck a rich vein of form; aided and abetted by some wonderful greenside bunker play and stout holing-out, he swept to victory in grand style. It was the first time the championship was seen on TV in colour, and Britain had a new sporting hero.

Jacklin had come a long way from his early days in Scunthorpe, Lincolnshire. His father had been a keen player, and although the family had modest means, through Jacklin's own efforts and the help of some good friends the opportunities for him to play and practise came along. He applied for and got the position as assistant professional to Bill Shankland, the professional at the Potters Bar Golf Club just north of the M25 in Hertfordshire, the beginning of a love–hate relationship between the two men. Shankland was a former Australian rugby league player and had competed in that sport at the very highest level; he was also a

pounds in the kitty, and his game improved rapidly. He met Vivienne, a charming girl from Belfast. They married, and it appeared to be a liaison made in heaven.

In July 1969 Jacklin arrived in Lytham with a good-looking CV, but there were a lot of awfully good players in the field and he certainly wasn't among the favourites. He struck the ball well, though, and whenever he got into trouble, mainly in greenside bunkers, he was absolutely brilliant, time and time again getting down in two from the sand. That was the key to his victory, plus the fact that he kept his nerve right to the last hole, where he struck a superb tee shot right down the middle, played a good second, and putted twice to become the champion – and well deserved it was.

He spent time in America, winning a couple of tournaments and rapidly growing in stature. In 1970 he played in the US Open Championship at Hazeltine, a new Robert Trent Jones-designed course in Minnesota, and a venue heavily criticised by many of the players who said it was far too immature and not by any stretch of the imagination ready to house such a prestigious

Trevino produced a miraculous shot at the penultimate hole, Jacklin three-putted from nowhere and made a mess of the last hole, and that was that.

first-class golfer, finishing in the top half dozen at the Open Championship on a couple of occasions. Jacklin said he was a very hard taskmaster, bordering on mean.

Whether that's true or not, under Shankland's tutelage Jacklin flourished. There were one or two members at the club who were also very supportive, so he managed to get some money together and started to play in a few tournaments. It wasn't long before there was a few thousand

event. Well, *they* might not have liked it but Jacklin certainly did. He won at a canter – two Open Championships within the space of twelve months.

He continued to play very well, but in 1972, when the Open was played at Muirfield, he was dealt a body blow. Lee Trevino and Jack Nicklaus were his main contenders that year, but Jacklin was surely going to win his second British Open with only a couple of holes to go. Trevino, seemingly out of it,

Above **Jacklin grits his teeth as a putt goes close at the English National Championship, September 1977** (© Empics).

Right **Open Champion 1969, Royal Lytham & St Annes** (© Popperfoto).

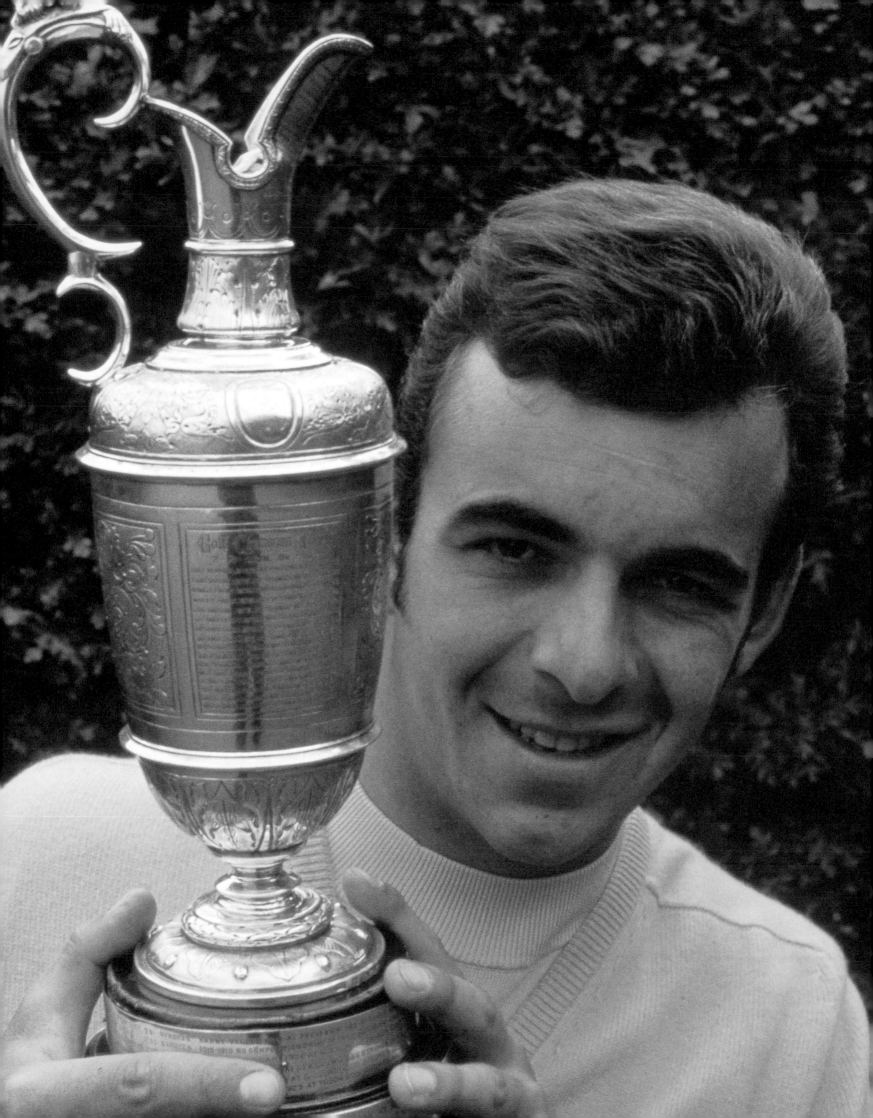

The cheeky chappie from Scunthorpe gave us hope, led us to wondrous victories in Ryder Cup matches and generally contributed much to the golfing scene.

Left **Waiting his turn to putt at 1999's Open Championship at Carnoustie (© Empics).**

Above **Taking a drop during the 1973 Ryder Cup at Muirfield (© Popperfoto).**

produced a miraculous shot at the penultimate hole, chipping in to to secure a par five, Jacklin three-putted from nowhere and made a mess of the last hole, and that was that. Trevino had won two Opens in a row, and Jacklin was crestfallen. He was even pipped to second place by Nicklaus.

Although he went on to win a number of events after that, the sparkle appeared to have gone. In all truth, I think Muirfield affected his nerves; he certainly started to complain about everything. Life had been unfair, Mark McCormack's management team, IMG, had not looked after him as well as they should have. There's no doubt he chased around the world earning large sums of money from various activities, bought a most magnificent house in the Cotswolds and lavished many thousands of pounds on it, and was also generous to members of his and his wife's family. Later on he did admit that he had been wrong and pointed the finger at IMG for not 'slowing him down'

and capitalising on his two Open Championship victories. He felt his hectic schedule contributed to his 'burn out' factor.

He and Vivienne moved to Jersey, where the tax laws were more relaxed, taking Vivienne's mother and father with them. After a number of years an opportunity arose for him to go and live and work in Spain, becoming the golf director at what is now the Valderrama Golf Club. He built a house alongside the 18th fairway and lived in fine style. But Jacklin, I'm sorry to say, appeared to want everyone to give him things for very little return. He was still a considerable figure in the world of golf, but was slowing down in terms of his golfing activities. His nerves were frayed, but all was not lost. The BBC offered him a TV contract to work on their golf coverage. He wasn't paid a fortune, but he had a platform which might lead to other things. Then Jacklin's world turned upside down when Vivienne tragically suffered a brain haemorrhage and sadly died.

At the 1969 Open Championship Jacklin swept to victory in grand style. Britain had a new sporting hero.

Above **Jacklin searches for his ball amongst Royal Birkdale's sand dunes, July 1971** (© Empics).

Right **Captain of the European team at the 1993 Ryder Cup matches** (© Empics).

He married a second time when he met and fell in love with Astrid, a charming Norwegian girl with whom he started another family. Then he had a falling-out with Jamie Patiño, owner of Valderrama, but almost immediately another opportunity offered itself. A new course, San Roque, had been created, and Jacklin went there as golf director. The Japanese owners were very pleased to secure his services, but for one reason or another he didn't make the most of it. Of course, according to Jacklin it was all 'their' fault. Commercial television offered him work and he left San Roque under a cloud, but, instead of saying kindly things about his time at the BBC, he was ungracious, foolishly slamming the door on any possible return.

At this stage he was telling everybody that he hated the game. His nerves were shot to hell and he was approaching 50, but he decided he would get himself into shape, battle his nerves and have a go on the American Senior Tour. He did reasonably well to begin with and won an event, but it was plain to see he was disenchanted with the game. His body language was poor on the course, he

hardly smiled and his shoulders slumped, so this rather grumpy figure did nothing to endear himself to the crowds or the powers-that-be. He was offered many chances by various people and organisations to move forward and in spite of himself he more than kept body and soul together, but whether it was through lack of direction or his own extravagances – in some cases, plain bad luck – his bank account was never as full as it should have been, which is a pity because despite his complaining nature he could be a good companion. He's certainly a very good interviewee, but it has to be said he never worked hard enough at any of the many opportunities that came his way.

He's artistic and a very good woodworker. He has two delightful families. He was, for a period, the flag bearer of British golf, our homegrown hero. Now, at times, he looks rather forlorn, but we should be thankful for those glorious years when the cheeky chappie from Scunthorpe gave us hope, led us to wondrous victories in Ryder Cup matches and generally contributed much to the golfing scene. It all went past much too soon.

BOBBY JONES

Above **Jones with his fifth and final US Amateur trophy, 1930** (© Popperfoto).

Right **Photographed in 1930, a year in which Jones won the US and British Opens, plus the US and British Amateur titles** (© Phil Sheldon).

Although Bobby Jones played his most famous competitive season more than 70 years ago, his name is still known and revered to this day. Whenever people gather to talk about the icons of the game, Jones is in everyone's top ten. When you consider that he played all his competitive golf as an amateur against the top professionals of the day and won thirteen major championships, his record is remarkable. And all that in an age when to play an event in Britain meant a minimum of 21 days' travel by car, rail and ship.

Bobby was the second child of Robert Purmedus Jones and Clara Merrick Thomas. They had had an earlier son, but he was very frail and lived for only three months. Jones didn't weigh much more than the first baby at birth, and his chances of survival looked very slight indeed. He had a very poor digestive system, his stomach rejected everything except egg white and bland vegetables, and the doctors thought it remarkable that he survived at all. He lived a very strange life, segregated from other small children for fear he would contract some germ which would end his life. It could be said that the climate of Atlanta in those far-off days before the advent of air-conditioning was not helpful to a child of a delicate constitution.

In 1907, when Jones was five, his parents took a house for the summer near the East Lake Golf Course. His mother and father took up the game, and it wasn't long before young Jones was knocking a ball about near his house with a cut-down golf club. Robert and Clara liked the district, and the following year they made it their home. By this time Jones had really got a taste for the game, even though he wasn't yet seven. He had no tutor as such, he just watched his mother and father swing the club, although he was befriended by the club professional, Jimmy Maiden. Originally from Carnoustie, Maiden had travelled to America at the turn of the century and was 'spreading the golfing gospel' along with his brother, Stewart.

By the time he was twelve Jones was scoring in the 70s. It was then he saw a match between Harry Vardon and Ted Ray, two great British professionals who were on an exhibition tour of the United States. He was impressed with Vardon's smooth swing, but he also enjoyed the way Ted Ray attacked the ball. The next year he played in the Southern Amateur Championship and reached the finals of the section for handicap players. By the age of fourteen, all signs of his earlier sickness having disappeared, Bobby was the club champion and featured in all the local events. Although under six feet in height, he had a solid build, broad shoulders and strong legs. His short game was quite remarkable. It seemed he was able to pitch the ball close to the hole from almost any position 50 or 60 yards from the green, and his putting was quite brilliant.

When Bobby was still fourteen his father entered him for the US Amateur Championship. This raised a few eyebrows, I can tell you. The championship that year was to be played at Merion; although a short course, it is one of the most testing to be found anywhere. He opened up with a 74 on the West Course and followed that with an horrendous 89 on the East, but still that was good enough to qualify for the matchplay stages where he was an immediate sensation. In the first round he beat Eben Byers, a former champion, by 3 & 2, and in the next round, even though he lost five out of the first six holes to Frank Dyer, he managed to win 4 & 2.

Going into the 36-hole matches his next opponent was the reigning champion, Bob Gardner. Jones was one up at lunch, but towards the end of the first nine that afternoon Gardner produced a string of beautiful shots to save pars. The fight went out of Jones and he displayed a rather petulant attitude, particularly when he halved or even lost holes he felt he deserved to win.

Above **Addressing the St Andrews crowd after winning the British Amateur title in 1930 (© Popperfoto).**

It was a long time before Jones became as good with matchplay as he was with a card and pencil. He was developing a dreadful temper which took him several years to get under control.

Although he had already won a number of major events, it was in 1930 that Jones achieved what many considered the impossible: he won the Open Championships of the United States and Great Britain and also their amateur titles. Then he decided to retire, at the tender age of 28 – a remarkable career crammed into just a few years. Among other things he was a fully qualified lawyer, and he put up his plate in his home town of Atlanta. He then decided to turn professional, tempted by Hollywood to make a series of instructional films which were extraordinary for the fact that they showed that Jones, contrary to many people's beliefs and theories, was very much an 'inside to out' player, a method which is pretty well shunned today, but he made it work brilliantly. Some years ago those films were

reprocessed with the help of modern technology and put out again on the open market. They sold in huge numbers, not only to golfing enthusiasts but also to collectors of golfing memorabilia.

Jones had made his first visit to Great Britain in 1921 when he was chosen to play for America in the Walker Cup match. It was his first taste of links golf, although Royal Liverpool, or Hoylake as it's better known, is not as 'linksy' as many other seaside courses. Jones played well in the matches and won both his foursomes and singles, but he was trounced in the fourth round of the Amateur Championship by Alan Graham, 6 & 5. He went on to play in the Open Championship at St Andrews where his temper was really unleashed, culminating in him tearing up his card and storming off the course. On his return to the United States he was heavily criticised. He felt ashamed, knowing his temper had let him down once more, but he didn't learn his lesson. He continued to throw clubs, and soon received

Whenever people gather to talk about the icons of the game, Jones is in everyone's top ten.

a letter from the United States Golf Association telling him he would not be allowed to play in their events, which included the US Open and Amateur Championship, unless he learnt to control his temper. In friendly play at East Lake near Atlanta he still threw clubs and used words no gentle Southern boy should know, but suddenly, when the big tournaments came along, he changed. He learnt to keep his head under control, and he never again threw a golf club in any form of competition.

It's interesting to note that at this time the Atlanta journalist O. B. Keeler, who went on to become one of the icons of golf writing, was given the brief to follow Jones wherever he went and report on his progress. Looking back on Jones' career, Keeler decided it neatly divided into two parts: the seven years when defeat followed defeat and the seven years when everything went right and victories were almost commonplace. Those lean years taught him how to win.

He won his first major championship in 1923 when he was just a few months past his twenty-first birthday, even though the last few holes were a torturous business, Jones making all sorts of elementary mistakes and finishing bogey, bogey, double bogey – four strokes lost in the final three

holes. His supporters were delighted when he finished, but Jones uttered the immortal words, 'I didn't finish like a champion, I finished like a yellow dog.' He always took great pride in his performance but hated making a fool of himself out on the golf course. Suddenly, though, the words of congratulations died in the supporters' mouth for Bobby Cruikshank came from nowhere, birdied the last hole and forced a play-off. And what a play-off it was. It went right down to the final shots, Jones striking an iron of such grandeur that it almost took the breath away. From a sandy lie, over water, a carry of at least 200 yards, he put it to within ten feet. Suddenly he was the Open champion of the United States.

He was off on an extraordinary run of form. Of his next six championships he won three, lost two play-offs and finished second. When he came to Britain he won every time he played, and for a spell of eight years in our two major championships, the Open and Amateur, Jones sustained a level of play no one before or since has ever approached.

Between 1923 and his retirement in 1930, he won the British Open three times, our Amateur Championship once, in 1930, the US Open Championship in 1923, 1926, 1929 and 1930, and the US Amateur in 1924, 1925, 1927, 1928 and 1930. In that short period he also came second in the US Open in 1924 and lost in a play-off by just one stroke in 1925 and 1928. Another point to consider is the fact that both Walter Hagen and Gene Sarazen were very much at the top of their games in the mid- to late 1920s. You can also throw in Tommy Armour, no slouch at the game.

Bobby's parents were justly proud of their son's golfing achievements and encouraged him all the way, his father in the early days, although not a rich man, paying some of the bills. In 1924, Bobby got married, but his wife didn't really fit into the golfing scene and in a way resented his worldwide fame. She may well have been a big factor in his decision to retire from competitive golf at such a young age.

When I look at the clubs and balls that were available at that time, I marvel at his skill, his scoring rate and his general prowess. The golf courses were nowhere near as manicured as they are today, the bunkers were unraked, but still he kept playing to a remarkable standard. He in fact found playing golf at the highest level a great

strain, and on many occasions was physically sick before going out to play – perhaps a legacy of those early days when his stomach was a delicate thing to say the least. Yet he is one of the very few golfers to have been honoured by having his image on a national stamp.

His law business flourished after retirement from golf, but soon he felt it was time to move on to other things. Along with his partner, New York banker Clifford Roberts, he founded the Augusta National Golf Club, where the Masters is played every year. He called on Alistair MacKenzie, who was making a considerable name for himself in the world of golf course architecture, to assist in the design, and all three in their different ways set about creating a magnificent golf course on a couple of hundred acres of undulating land on the edge of the proud city of Augusta in the state of Georgia. There was already a fine old plantation house and some ancillary buildings on the plot, together with a fine selection of trees, as the land had recently been used as a tree and turf nursery. They could never, of course, have imagined the Masters would grow into such a wondrous event. The main railway from New York to Florida passed close by, and the original concept was simply to create a golf course where lovers of the game and like-minded souls could meet in the early spring to escape the rigours of winters in the north-east. The baseball teams went down to Florida for their pre-season warm-ups, so the journalists who doubled on covering baseball and golf could spend a few pleasant days in convivial company, golfing and getting ready for the coming season.

Jones was the most famous golfer of his time, so he had no trouble in encouraging the top players of the day to compete in his modest event staged early in the season. The partners were lucky, too: in 1935, only the second year of the tournament, Gene Sarazen pulled off an outrageous coup by holing his second shot at the par-five 15th. He played the last three holes in fine style, and suddenly, out of the blue, he'd won. The top journalists of the day were on hand to record this feat and the legend of 'The Masters' was born, although it struggled in its early days and was on the verge of bankruptcy on a number of occasions. It must have been a great sadness for many that Roberts and Jones fell out in later years, particularly as Jones had been struck down by the most vicious form of arthritis which forced him to spend his last years totally incapacitated in a wheelchair. Roberts did not attend his funeral, which upset some members of the family. In later years he took his own life, shooting himself in the head on the bank by the 9th green of the short course.

Many find it hard to understand how an 'ordinary' golf club is able to run one of the world's major sporting events with no help from any other large organisation. Think, for instance, about the events in football, rugby, cricket, hockey, squash, American football, baseball, basketball, motor racing and many other sports, all of which employ a huge number of behind-the-scenes operatives to bring everything to fruition. Well, Augusta National *appears* to do it all by itself, but strictly speaking that isn't true. They've softened their ways over the years, and now the US Professional Tour plays a big part in the running of the event, although it would be totally wrong to think that the club isn't very much in a 'hands on' situation. Nothing is altered or gets done without their consent.

As a young boy I caddied for Bobby Jones at the Parkstone Golf Club during what proved to be one of his last games in England. He played with my father, Percy, Reggie Whitcombe, the club professional who had won the Open Championship in 1938, and Frank McInnes, whose parents used to own the famous Dormy Hotel which sits alongside the Ferndown Golf Club where my father was the professional for many years. Jones, despite wearing his service uniform and not having the advantage of proper golf shoes, struck the ball beautifully and was absolutely charming. He was a heavy smoker, and some of the stories about his drinking are, to say the least, memorable. All in all a remarkable man whose strike rate in terms of winning major championships may never be beaten. Maybe not even by Tiger Woods.

There have been many glowing tributes written about Bobby Jones, none nicer than these words from author and non-golfer Paul Gallico: 'He was a gentleman and there was laughter in his heart and on his lips and he loved his friends. He was the best golf player the world had ever known, a fine decent human being.'

Fine words indeed for perhaps the greatest player ever seen.

Above **At St Andrews in 1958, aged 56** (© Popperfoto).

Pages 66 & 67 When I look at the clubs and balls that were available at that time, I marvel at his skill (© Allsport).

Jones was developing a dreadful temper which took him several years to get under control.

BOBBY LOCKE

Above **Bobby Locke had a swing all his own** (© Popperfoto).

Right **Locke won the first of his four British Open titles at Sandwich in 1949** (© Empics).

Some of you may be wondering why I've included Bobby Locke in my list of golfing heroes. Well, the answer is quite simple: he was a superstar. Perhaps an unlikely looking one, but how I wish someone with his temperament and skills was around today, just for the fun of seeing how they would measure up and compete under modern conditions. In these pages I speak of Lee Trevino's set-up and style, aiming way to the left, ball well forward, trying to eliminate the left-hand side of the course, cutting the ball back towards the fairway. Locke was the exact opposite. Playing with a closed stance and aiming well to the right, he took the club back on the inside and had a huge shoulder turn, and from there looped it back until, almost unbelievably, everything was correct when the club head reached the ball. He was very much a right-handed player, which meant hooking, feared by most players. In Trevino's words, 'You can talk to a fade but a hook won't listen.'

But that was how Locke played the game, a looping flight moving at least 45 degrees back to the fairway. He could draw the ball with anything, and had an amazing ability to play short irons on to hard greens and get his ball to land limply with virtually no bounce, fire or spring. How he managed to do that I never discovered. He was a wonderful judge of distance, and it was all done by eye. There was no pacing the course for Bobby Locke. Sometimes in exhibition matches, and I played dozens with Locke when I was a young man, he'd take a card off the bar in the clubhouse and discover halfway down the first fairway that he'd got a ladies card, so the yardage was all up the spout. He continued to look at it as though it was giving him great knowledge – which, of course, it wasn't – and happily played the most beautifully controlled shots virtually level with the flag every time. I don't think I ever saw Locke go charging through the back of a green in all the time he and I golfed together.

Over the years Locke put on a considerable amount of weight but still retained a great degree of suppleness. His rhythm remained the same throughout his career; everything he did was done at a set pace. I never saw him hurry because he always allowed himself time. Whether it was getting up in the morning, getting dressed, having breakfast or getting to the golf course, he seemed utterly relaxed, but we were to discover later that that was far from being a natural air: he always took a couple of Veganin tablets, the smart aspirin of the day. I don't think they actually did anything physically, but they certainly lent him a feeling of confidence and well-being.

Apart from Locke's ability to keep the ball on the fairway from the tee and judge distance to perfection, his greatest strength was on the green. His thoughts were pretty much the same when putting or driving. He gripped the club very gently and saw the ball move slightly right to left into the hole, again at the perfect speed. He reckoned that if he achieved that pace there were three sides into the hole. His two heroes were Bobby Jones and Walter Hagen, who had given him some putting tips when they met in South Africa in the mid-1930s. I don't think anybody struck a putt quite as purely as Locke.

He always talked about imparting topspin and how important that was to get the ball running smoothly. Scientists, however, have proved that is not possible, that all putts 'leave' the ground for a split-second after they've been struck so all begin their journey with backspin. If the strike has imparted any slice or hook spin to the ball, that dissipates itself once the ball starts rolling at its optimum speed. No matter, Locke believed what he believed, and the power of the mind can be stronger than scientific proof. Perhaps his method of striking put less backspin on the ball and was one of the reasons why his ball ran so far with just the gentlest of hits. In my book, he was the

great bunker player – in that department he was, in fact, quite clumsy – he was a master chipper, the strange thing being that if the ball was only a foot or so off the green he still used one of his three most lofted clubs. I never saw him use a putter when not actually on the green. He moved his body a huge amount during those little shots, but the ball ran unerringly towards the hole. Oh, what a glorious feel he had for those little chips!

Locke's family originally came from Northern Ireland, setting up home in South Africa round about the turn of the last century. He had one sister, three years older than him. Locke always said his was a very happy upbringing, and it was his father who encouraged him to play and enjoy the game. He first arrived in Britain in the late 1930s while still an amateur. He was very slim then (how that was to change over the years!), perhaps South Africa's best player. He wasn't long but he was reliable, and some say he began his career playing with a fade. On those sun-baked fairways in South Africa he got enough length from that shot, but not in Great Britain, so he decided he would try to get draw on the ball, thereby hoping to get more run on his tee shots without necessarily hitting the ball harder.

Round about 1938 Locke abandoned his amateur career and turned professional. In those days you just couldn't announce your intentions, turn pro and start immediately on a new career, you had to serve an apprenticeship. However, one of the few events he was allowed to play in was the Irish Open, which he won, his first success outside South Africa. He also played in the last Open Championship at St Andrews before the Second World War and, although he didn't win, he made a lot of friends. He joined the South African Air Force, flew Liberators between Canada, the United States and Great Britain – ferry pilots, they were known as – and hardly played any golf for two and a half years.

I don't know whether or not it was his wartime diet, but on demobilisation he arrived to play in his first tournaments weighing close on fifteen stones. In 1946 he won three tournaments and finished joint runner-up in the Open behind Sam Snead, whom he invited to South Africa for a series of exhibition matches. Snead was probably the best golfer in the world at that time (Byron Nelson had retired and Ben Hogan had not yet quite

Above **Locke strolls down one of Walton Heath's fairways with Frank Jowle during the** *News of the World* **Matchplay Championship, September 1952 (© Empics).**

greatest putter ever. It didn't matter what the surface was like, he just rolled them in. He never spent an awful lot of time up and down the line. Locke would simply examine the ground three or four feet short of the hole to see where the ball might deviate one way or t'other as it died towards the hole.

He was a one-off. I don't think anybody ever tried to copy his style. He used the same hickory-shafted rusty-bladed putter for many years. I was privileged to have a few putts with it on a number of occasions, and the moment it was in your hands you had the same feeling a violinist must get when allowed to hold a Stradivarius. When you put the club behind the ball you felt it wanted to swing the way the master swung it – eerie. Although not a

'Very early in my career I realised that putting was half the game of golf. No matter how well I might play the long shots, if I couldn't putt I would never win!'
BOBBY LOCKE

Right **Shaking Harry Bradshaw's hand after the pair's monumental head-to-head at the 1949 British Open** (© Popperfoto).

Above **Yet another putt disappears, May 1956** (© Empics).

emerged). He agreed to the matches and Locke won the series by twelve matches to two, which convinced him he should go off to the United States. Snead was shattered and christened Locke 'droopy jowls'. He just couldn't believe how this strange-looking golfer could have beaten him so badly. Much of the time Snead's second shots were inside Locke's, but time and time again Locke's putting destroyed him. Locke actually asked Snead if he should go to the States – did he think he'd be able to make a living there? 'Make a living?' replied Snead. 'You'll get rich, and very quickly.' So off he went to try his luck.

His first appearance was at the Masters in 1947, where he created quite a stir. One of the pundits remarked, 'The old guy [Locke was only 30] has the worst swing I've ever seen, his wrists so floppy,

dammit, they remind me of a pyjama cord.' Pyjama cord or not, he managed fourteenth place, and in his next four tournaments he finished first, first, third and first. That last victory caused quite a fuss. Hogan was ahead of the pack by five after two rounds, a seemingly unassailable lead, but Locke went about his business in his own quiet way and won with four strokes to spare. The Americans decided that the guy from the jungle had a game after all. He went round the course in a cocoon of concentration, hardly speaking to anybody. Spectators were allowed on the fairway in those days, and how well I remember Locke's voice ringing out, 'Through, please! Through, please!' I think those were the only words he ever spoke. He achieved a record during that first year that has never been beaten by an overseas golfer,

'He was the greatest putter I have ever seen. He'd hit a 50-footer and before the ball got halfway he'd be tipping his hat to the crowd. He wore out his hats tipping them.'

SAM SNEAD ON

BOBBY LOCKE

winning seven times and ending up in the money list just behind Jimmy Demaret, who had played the whole year. He also won one of the great unofficial events of the day, the Tam O' Shanter Tournament, sponsored by a Chicago businessman. The prize was $7,000, and it was rumoured Locke also received an appearance fee of $5,000. If that's true, $12,000 in 1947 was an unholy amount of money.

Back he went to South Africa, but he returned to the US the following year, winning three events and doing very well in a number of others. One of his victories was again in Chicago where he won by a margin of sixteen strokes, which set a US Tour record. But there was growing resentment among American players, both for his success and the high appearance money he was said to be collecting. What did they do? Well, they banned him from playing on the Tour under the pretext that he had failed to turn up for two events for which he had been entered. Many Americans thought this was disgraceful, and, although it was soon lifted, the ban left a sour taste in Locke's mouth and he competed less frequently. He had proved himself in the States and was now far happier competing in Britain and Europe.

His main target was the British Open, and when the championship was held in 1949 at the Royal St George's Golf Club he was installed as the firm favourite. Of course his deeds in America had not gone unnoticed, even though in those far-off days there were far fewer golfing magazines than there are today and golf reporters were fairly thin on the ground. Television was non-existent. Locke played well, but a mistake here and there showed he was human. The man who stole the headlines that year was Irishman Harry Bradshaw, a wonderful portly figure with a roly-poly gait, a grip where practically every finger of his right hand overlapped the left, a truly agricultural swing but a wonderful ability to strike the ball time and again out of the middle of the club face, and a putting stroke to die for. It was definitely a method all his own.

It was here at Royal St George's in 1949 that the famous broken bottle incident took place. At the 5th hole Bradshaw's ball came to rest against some broken glass. In those days golfers seldom asked for a ruling; the officials were miles away in the clubhouse anyway, so invariably you just got on

with it. Harry gave the ball (and the glass) a whack and was lucky not to do himself any damage. It definitely unsettled him, and he finished that particular round rather poorly.

Come the final day, and what a wonderful day it was: the sun shone and the golf was sparkling. Bradshaw had set the pace and Locke had to finish par, par, par (three, four, four) to tie. In fact, he finished four, three, four to force a play-off over 36 holes. Locke was coldly determined and played the first eighteen quite magnificently, going round in 67 to Bradshaw's 74. He carried on in much the same vein in the afternoon and didn't have a five on his card until the 33rd, and at the end of the day he won by twelve strokes. He defended his title at Royal Troon the following year.

I have to smile when I think of Locke's preparation for a tournament round. He never used to practise on the putting green, believing the texture bore no resemblance to the actual greens. His philosophy was that wherever he was on the 1st hole, he used that first putt to get the 'feel' of the green. If the ball fell in for a birdie, all well and good. He'd just tuck it away in his back pocket and move on to the next hole.

He had a wonderful old caddy called Bill Golder. At the Open at St Andrews in 1957 I was coming back from the beach where I'd been hitting some balls off the compacted sand only to see Golder standing by the side of the road about 100 yards from the clubhouse fishing half a dozen balls out of a huge Slazenger golf bag. There was a patch of rough grass there about eight feet by three feet and a drop of about eight feet down on to the sand where the Swilken Burn emptied into the sea. I was chatting to Golder when the great man arrived. I liked Bobby enormously and I think he enjoyed my youthful company. We chatted about things, he was right at the top of the leaderboard and there was much to do that day. After a few minutes I looked at my watch and said, 'Well, I must be off.' Now, this was long before the days when leaders were placed out last, so Bobby asked me what the time was. I told him, and he replied, 'Oh well, time to go, then.' Golder, in the meantime, had clambered down over the rocks and was some 100 yards down the beach waiting for his master to hit a few wedge shots. Locke had simply wanted to loosen up his muscles before he set off for the 1st tee. I'll never forget watching him wave Golder in

Above **The fourth and final claret jug, St Andrews, 1957** (© Popperfoto).

Pages 76 & 77 **Preparing for the 1949 Open Championship at Sandwich with a drive from the 18th tee. Frank Stranahan is closest to Locke** (© Popperfoto).

and then saunter back to the clubhouse with me. Having not hit a single practice shot, he went on to win the claret jug!

When it came to dress, Bobby was a creature of routine. He always wore the same clothes throughout his professional career: white buckskin shoes with leather soles, navy blue plus fours, long hand-knitted off-white stockings, a white shirt with collar and cuffs, a club tie of some sort – often an Air Force or South African PGA tie, or one that had been presented to him when he had been made an honorary member of a golf club, of which there were many in the UK – and a Cambridge Blue cashmere sweater, all topped off with a white peak cap. It was an interesting attitude for a number of reasons. When the press wrote about him they always described his attire, and it made travelling easier and clothes selection a matter of great simplicity.

In the late 1950s Locke was coming to the end of his best years. Peter Thomson was now well established, having won the three previous Open Championships from 1954 to 1956, and there was also Gary Player, who was making monumental strides in the world of golf and taking over Bobby's South African mantle. I like to think that Thomson admired Locke, but I always sensed there was a little bit of needle on both sides. Locke, being the older by some thirteen years, was perhaps mindful of the young master usurping his throne.

Without being unkind, Bobby had looked 55 since he was 30, and his 1957 victory at St Andrews was to be his last at this level. He had always planned to retire relatively early anyway. With the money he had won in the United States, he purchased a block of flats in Yeoville, a smart suburb of Johannesburg, as his security, his old-age pension. Sadly, his retirement did not go well. While travelling in his car he was struck by a train on an ungated railway crossing and was lucky to survive.

He was never the same afterwards, though. He lost the sight in his left eye and the accident also slightly affected his brain. He became very repetitive, but still retained his fine sense of humour and enjoyed nothing more than playing golf with friends or, indeed, acquaintances picked up along the way. The only problem was, a gentle round of golf could take you five or six hours because he kept stopping, talking, sitting down, telling another story, going into the halfway house, having tea and a round of sandwiches. All in all, though, if it was your first experience of being with the great man, it was something you never forgot.

Bobby was married to Mary, a Canadian lady of substantial proportions, and they produced a sparky daughter who championed her father's cause for many a year. Bobby died in 1987. Sadly, his wife and daughter slipped into great eccentricity and a few years ago committed suicide. They had been dead for several days when they were found barricaded in the block of flats at Yeoville. The smart suburb, once an elite part of town, had deteriorated greatly. They had strived to sell the property but nobody was interested, so they decided to end their lives together – a sad end to the story of one of the best competitors I ever saw.

Above **No doubt another beautifully judged approach shot, Wentworth, May 1958 (© Popperfoto).**

'Everyone examines greens. But only he knows what he's looking for.'
BEN HOGAN ON BOBBY LOCKE

JOHNNY MILLER

FACT FILE

FULL NAME: John Laurence Miller

BORN: 29 April 1947;
San Francisco, California, USA

TOURNAMENT WINS: 29
USA 24
Europe 3
Other 2

MAJORS: 2
Masters 0 (T2nd 1971; T2nd 1975; T2nd 1981)
US Open 1 (1973)
The Open 1 (1976)
US PGA 0 (T11th 1977)

US MONEY LIST WINS: 1
1974

RYDER CUP RECORD:
Appearances & Team Wins (W) 2 (1975–81/2W)
Matches (Won-Lost-Halved) 6 (2–2–2)
Wins (Singles-Foursomes-Fourballs) 2 (0–2–0)

Above & right **In the
early 1970s, Johnny Miller
looked, and was, a star**
(© Popperfoto and Empics).

Pages 80 & 81 **Surveying
the 12th green at Troon with
Tom Weiskopf, July 1973**
(© Popperfoto).

There was a time in the early 1970s when Johnny Miller strode the fairways of the world like a colossus. I remember having a conversation with him during the middle of his amazing streak and asking him what was going on. He replied, 'I really don't know, I really can't explain it, but when I stand over a shot I can "see" the result before I've played. I can see it sailing away into the distance.' Time and time again it happened just like that. His iron shots were fantastic and he putted like a demon, although he had rather a quick, jabby stroke which failed him in the end when his nerves got a little frayed, but he put together some amazing scores and for a time was winning five, six, seven tournaments a year, particularly in the early part of the season.

His playing career at the very top of the tree on the main Tour ended fairly quickly. Some say the rot set in when he bought a large property in the country and decided to work on the estate during the off season, putting in hours of hard, physical work. He altered his muscle structure through swinging pick-axes and sledgehammers for hours on end, erecting fences and the like. Whether this is true or not I don't know, but something happened. Almost overnight he lost his magic touch. I don't know if you've ever carried a couple of heavy suitcases for 75 or 100 yards, then put them down and tried to do something delicate. Your touch and feel definitely desert you and it takes a considerable amount of time before your body settles down again. One of Henry Cotton's tips years ago was never to carry your own clubs, or even pick up your set, at least 45 minutes prior to tee-off, because if you did it would alter your 'feel'. So I guess there could be something in it. There was, however, another good reason: he got the yips on the greens.

Miller moved into television where he very quickly carved a unique niche for himself,

attracting a lot of criticism from his fellow pros. Why? Well, he was actually critical of their play, cynical, sardonic and, on occasion, sneering. He managed to work in a sort of half-laughing tone when someone had played a particularly poor shot. But at least he sailed a straight course and never changed, and he remains one of the most popular, if controversial, commentators on American golf.

He was seduced some years ago to come out of retirement and play in the AT&T Tournament, the old Bing Crosby event, at Pebble Beach in the early part of the season. Oh, there was some gloating and smirking when they heard he'd found the nerve, the arrogance, the cheek to enter! After all he'd said about them, to go out and risk playing in this exalted company on a difficult golf course with thousands watching at the venue and millions at home on television! To his eternal credit, despite one or two shaky moments he won the damned thing, which stopped the chatter of many of his critics, but he had the good sense not to try it again.

I suppose in other sports players get spells when whatever they do is miraculous, then it's gone. Rugby, soccer, cricket, darts, snooker, any sport you can think of has had its fair share of competitors doing wondrous things, as if touched by a sporting god. Some have tried to analyse it in an effort to preserve those moments but have fallen by the wayside, some just rode their luck only to see it gradually disappear. Others wake up one morning to find that all their magical deeds appear to have been just a glorious dream. Miller was perhaps in that last category, but for a time it was certainly a joy to see this tall, blond-haired, athletic figure striding the fairways, hitting those wonderful iron shots into the heart of the green and leaving the rest of us trailing in his wake. He looked, and was, a star.

COLIN MONTGOMERIE

Born in Glasgow on 23 June 1963, Montgomerie is one of the youngest players featured in this book and he hasn't yet won a major championship, but he deserves to be here for a number of reasons. To win seven consecutive Orders of Merit on the European Tour is a mind-boggling achievement. Some unkind pundits remarked at the time that he was virtually playing in the second division, but I take exception to those remarks. The scores Montgomerie was producing day in and day out on very different golf courses were quite staggering.

He was fortunate to spend some of his early years alongside one of the great golf courses in Great Britain, Royal Troon, where his father was the club secretary. Having the opportunity to hone one's skills on such a formidable course, particularly if you're enjoying the game, is surely a great advantage. Bearing that in mind, it's strange to think that he hasn't performed well in our Open Championship which should, in all honesty, be his forte.

Colin should certainly have won at least one, if not two major championships in his time. One in

always felt his turn would come, but in 1997 he was pipped to the post yet again by Ernie Els, the actions of the crowd (or his own personal demons) playing a big role in his mini collapse over the final couple of holes.

I'm often asked if I think Montgomerie will ever win a major. Well, of course he might, but first he's got to overcome his largely self-created pressures. He deserves a championship, but I'm not a believer in that old saying – originating, it is said, from Ben Hogan – that anyone can win one major but it takes a helluva good player to win two. There are a number of players who have won two major championships and by no stretch of the imagination can they be called 'great' players, they just happened to strike it lucky at the correct moment, hole a couple of putts and, bingo, there they were holding the prized trophy aloft.

Over the past few years Colin's home life has come under very close scrutiny. It appears that his nomadic life was taking its toll on the family and all was not well in the Montgomerie household. That surely is a common shortcoming in modern

'I see it as a back-handed compliment. The hecklers obviously see me as a threat.'
MONTY, 1998

Above **Monty with the Volvo PGA trophy, May 1999 (© Empics).**

Right **Chipping from the sand at Carlsbad's 17th during the World of Golf Championship, February 2000 (© Popperfoto).**

particular comes to mind, the 1995 US PGA Championship at the Riviera Country Club in Los Angeles, California, where he was outrageously pipped to the post by the Australian Steve Elkington. On two occasions he came very close to winning the US Open, once being involved in a play-off with Ernie Els, the eventual winner, and Loren Roberts. He could well have done better there, but in all truth all three players started off appallingly in that eighteen-hole play-off. One

marriages, though I'm not saying it was better or worse years ago, or that women then were more prepared to put up with their husbands being away. I'm going back to the days when women ran the home, looked after the children and made them aware of the ways of the world – 'the hand that rocks the cradle rules the world'. I think it's the most important, rewarding, wondrous job to be 'there' bringing up a family, and it's probably the most difficult job in the world, particularly if

'A major won't change anything. If it comes, it's a bonus. It would be a relief more than anything. But I can look back at what I've achieved in Europe and be very, very happy.' MONTY

Left The 2001 Masters at Augusta. Monty strides out on the 16th fairway, closely followed by caddy Alastair McLean. The pair parted company in May 2002 (© Popperfoto).

Pages 86 & 87 Monty at the 1997 US PGA at Winged Foot (© Popperfoto).

Above **With his wife Eimair at Royal Ascot, 2000 (© Empics).**

your husband is away. But many husbands have been away for a variety of reasons, not just because of their job. I'm old enough to remember periods of war during which some husbands and wives didn't see each other for five or six years. Just imagine the strains *that* would place on a relationship.

But I'm not here to pontificate about the marital state of professional sportsmen and women, I simply view from afar and marvel at their skills. In my own way I'm delighted that the Montgomeries seem to have got their home life back on an even keel. It would be an awful waste if, after just a few short years of enormous success and accumulation of much gold, things should crumble and fall apart, even though we know it's happened many

times before, and on most occasions it's very painful, with recriminations and great feelings of guilt.

I certainly don't think Colin Montgomerie should feel guilty about not having won one of the world's majors so far. So what if he never does? He's left his mark on the world of professional golf and he's got many admirers who enjoy his openness – which sometimes is perhaps a little too honest for his own good. I've always enjoyed his company and watching him perform on the golf course, even when he has behaved like a tiresome baby throwing his toys out of the pram. And if that's the worst thing anyone can say about Colin, then all is not doom and gloom. I shall be the first to raise my glass if, in the years ahead, his name is engraved on one of the world's four major trophies.

BYRON NELSON

FACT FILE

FULL NAME: John Byron Nelson, Jr

BORN: 12 February 1912; Fort Worth, Texas

TOURNAMENT WINS: 66
USA 52
Europe 1
Other 13

MAJORS: 5
Masters 2 (1937; 1942 after play-off)
US Open 1 (1939 after playoff)
The Open 0 (5th 1937)
US PGA 2 (1940; 1945)

US MONEY LIST WINS: 2
1944; 1945 (awarded War Bonds for both wins)

RYDER CUP RECORD:
Appearances & Team Wins (W) 2 (1937–47/2W);
non-playing captain 1965 (1W)
Matches (Won-Lost-Halved) 4 (3–1–0)
Wins (Singles-Foursomes) 3 (1–2)

A very good case could be put forward that Byron Nelson is the greatest player the world has ever seen. Unarguably there was a period when he was the best, but his reputation has suffered with the passing of time. His amazing record is often dismissed by those who insist he didn't win enough major championships to be counted alongside the greats and that his career was far too short. Furthermore, Nelson wasn't called up during the war; it was said he was a haemophiliac. That description is not strictly true, but he did have a condition which made his blood slow to clot and he was ruled out of active service. His detractors also seized on this as a reason for his success: he won most of his tournaments when his main competitors were doing their service.

But let's examine the facts. Nelson's first major victory was the Masters in 1937. He'd won other tournaments and played in a Ryder Cup match

Nelson began his career using a 1.62 golf ball, the size championed in Great Britain and the one in general use at that time. It wasn't until 1931 that America brought in the larger 1.68 golf ball. However, the 1.62 clung on in Britain for more than 40 years. Steel shafts were also coming on to the scene. Nelson was the first golfer to fully adapt to both these huge advancements. He was a tall man, played with his arms very close to his body and was inclined to dip his knees as he came into the shot, but he was one of the straightest hitters the game's ever seen and wonderfully accurate, which helped to compensate for the fact that he was not one of the world's great putters.

Perhaps too much is made of Nelson's complete dominance of the world of golf between 1944 and 1946, but there is no doubt that the number of victories he recorded in those two years is staggering. One year he won eleven tournaments

Imagine being away from competitive golf for several years, entering a 'proper' tournament and finishing in the first half dozen!

prior to that, and had added four more majors by the time he retired, in 1946 at the age of 33, saying that he was tired of cocktail parties, speeches, lunches, travelling and generally being a superstar. Byron's wife Louise might well have been an influence in all this for she was a home lover, she didn't care for travel and hated her husband being away from home. Byron loved Louise deeply and in many ways felt he had nothing left to prove come the war's end. Then again, although he was so brilliant at golf, he did suffer from nerves, finding eating and sleeping very difficult before even relatively modest events.

in a row, had a little break, then continued on his merry way winning seven more – eighteen in all, for total prize money of $63,000, paid in war bonds. 'No opposition!' was the chant regularly heard from the golfing paparazzi, though in August of 1945 Ben Hogan had been discharged from the US Air Force. Nelson still won ten tournaments that year, though Hogan beat that figure by three. 'There was no pressure, few spectators, no television cameras, he wasn't being pulled from pillar to post by the press' came the cries. OK, maybe not, but imagine competing in all those events, some 25 or 26 in all, and coming out

Above **American Ryder Cup captain, 1965** (© Popperfoto).

Right **A charming, gentle, good man, and a very fine golfer** (© Allsport).

with an average of a fraction over 68 shots per round, as Nelson did, a figure beaten only by Tiger Woods in 2000. If you take into account the equipment at his disposal, the condition of the golf courses, etc., you must agree this was a remarkable spell of golf.

Elsewhere in these pages I mention Jack Nicklaus' wonderful 64 at Augusta in 1965, but years before Nelson registered a round of 66 in which he hit every green in one or two and took 34 putts with just two one-putt greens, and they were both tap-ins of under two feet. Nelson was very meticulous in everything he did and kept a little book in which he wrote down every round he played, going over it time and time again to see where he'd slipped up, where something had gone wrong and how it could be improved upon.

People today are unduly influenced by the

longevity of Jack Nicklaus' career. Like Old Father Thames, he just kept rolling along. But how long is long enough? If your criteria *is* longevity, then players such as Bobby Jones, Ben Hogan, Johnny Miller and Tony Jacklin, not to mention Byron Nelson, probably wouldn't feature in your magic circle. I like to think that Nelson retired because he'd just had enough. Perhaps some of his nerve had gone; certainly the all-consuming desire to win had long disappeared. Like Bobby Locke after his victory in the Open Championship in 1957, all passion for the game, at that level, had been spent. Much is also made of the fact that Nelson didn't make an awful lot of money during his career, yet somehow he managed to purchase a thousand-acre ranch just outside Fort Worth, Texas, where he raised pedigree cattle with great success.

Some more unkind people said that after his

Below **Receiving the Ryder Cup in 1965 from Prime Minister Harold Wilson** (© Popperfoto).

A very good case could be put forward that Byron Nelson is the greatest player the world has ever seen.

Nelson suffered from nerves, finding eating and sleeping very difficult before even relatively modest events.

Right **Nelson was a tall man and played with his arms very close to his body** (© Phil Sheldon).

retirement he attempted to make several comebacks. I disagree, although he did enter a tournament from time to time when it suited him, setting even more remarkable records. Imagine being away from competitive golf for several years, entering a 'proper' tournament and finishing in the first half dozen! In 1951 Bing Crosby coaxed Nelson to come and play in his tournament at Pebble Beach. As always there was a very strong field, but, lo and behold, he won. Then there were his annual appearances at the Masters, where he continued to play some good, sound golf; in later years he appeared every April alongside Gene Sarazen and Sam Snead acting as one of the honorary starters, playing the first nine holes much to the delight of the huge galleries. And in 1955 he took his wife on a holiday to Europe, discovered the French Open Championship was being played at La Boulie, a delightful golf course on the outskirts of Paris, entered and won. The first prize was only about £300 but I'm sure it went a long way towards covering his holiday expenses. On the last day of that French Open he played with my dear friend David Thomas, who marvelled at Nelson's ball-striking ability.

He befriended several young players: two of the best amateurs of the day, Harvie Ward and Frank Stranahan, and professionals Tony Lema, Ken Venturi and Bobby Nichols, all winners of major championships. But by far his most famous pupil was Tom Watson, who bears many of the hallmarks of his mentor. He went on to captain the US Ryder Cup team when the matches were played at Royal Birkdale in 1965, where I had some success partnering Christie O'Connor in the foursomes and fourballs, scoring five points out of six. Nelson was very complimentary and spoke fondly of his memories of my father, Percy, whom he'd met in Ryder Cup competition in the late 1930s. For a time Nelson was also employed by the ABC television company and covered many golf events. He had his own homespun type of delivery and produced many 'Nelsonisms', quirky statements that brought many a smile.

He's rather frail these days, having had hip replacements which have worked reasonably well. Sadly he can't play golf any more, though he still does a little bit of chipping and putting. I'm sure that for as long as he can he'll see the start of play on the first day at Augusta. A charming, gentle, good man, and a very fine golfer.

Below **Nelson with Harry Weetman, captain of Britain's Ryder Cup team, Royal Birkdale, 1965** (© Popperfoto).

Right **Nelson was one of the straightest hitters the game's ever seen, and wonderfully accurate** (© Allsport).

He retired in 1946 at the age of 33, saying he was tired of cocktail parties, speeches, lunches, travelling and generally being a superstar.

JACK NICKLAUS

FACT FILE

FULL NAME: Jack William Nicklaus

BORN: 21 January 1941; Columbus, Ohio

TOURNAMENT WINS: 84
USA 70
Europe 4
Other 10
US Seniors 10

MAJORS: 18(20)
Masters 6 (1963; 1965; 1966 after play-off; 1972; 1975; 1986)
US Open 4 (1962 after play-off; 1967; 1972; 1980)
The Open 3 (1966; 1970 after play-off; 1978)
US PGA 5 (1963; 1971; 1973; 1975; 1980)
US Amateur 2 (1959; 1961)
  US Senior Open 2 (1991 after play-off; 1993)
  PGA Seniors 1 (1991)

US MONEY LIST WINS: 8
1964; 1965; 1967; 1971; 1972; 1973; 1975; 1976

HIGHEST WORLD RANKING: 19
During 1986 – the first year of ranking

WALKER CUP RECORD:
Appearances & Team Wins (W) 2 (1959–61/2W)
Matches (Won-Lost-Halved) 4 (4–0–0)
Wins (Singles-Foursomes) 4 (2–2)

RYDER CUP RECORD:
Appearances & Team Wins (W) 6 (1969–81/5W);
captain (non-playing) 1983, 1987(1W)
Matches (Won-Lost-Halved) 28 (17–8–3)
Wins (Singles-Foursomes-Fourballs) 17 (4–8–5)

PRESIDENTS CUP RECORD:
Appearances & Team Wins (W)
captain (non-playing) 1998 (0W)

Above **Keeping a tight grip on the claret jug, 1978 (© Empics).**

Right **Waving to the crowd on his final appearance at the British Open, St Andrews, 2000 (© Empics).**

The Nicklaus family originally came from Alsace-Lorraine, an area of the continent forever being battled over by France and Germany. The product of a comfortably middle-class home, Jack began to play golf at the age of ten, encouraged all the way by his father, Charlie, who owned a pharmacy which within the space of twenty years or so had grown into a group of four. Jack was not an athletic child, being relatively short and very stocky. Even into his late twenties he remained a relatively unattractive physical specimen, huge of thigh and small of hand with a mop of flaxen hair cut to a height of a quarter of an inch. He might not have been a figure of great beauty, but he certainly had something when it came to playing the game of golf.

By the time he was twelve he'd broken 80, and over the next 50 years I don't think he took more than 79 on many occasions. He had a big, wide swing for his height but the smallness of his hands decreed he should either use a double-handed grip or one where the little finger of the right hand

1959, beating one of the country's finest golfers, Charlie Coe, by one hole. It was a magnificent final. He was picked that year to play in the Walker Cup and had his first taste of links golf at Muirfield, twenty miles to the east of Edinburgh, winning both his foursomes and singles matches.

He played electrifying golf. He'd learnt to control his great power and when under pressure was a supreme holer of putts in the ten- to fifteen-foot range. Strangely enough he never became a great chipper or bunker player. His power, majestic long-iron play and sound putting were his main assets, but perhaps the finest of all was his golfing brain. I don't think Nicklaus ever hit a shot before he was ready. Many people thought he was a slow player. In fact there was a period when the authorities challenged him every week, continually having a go at his snail-like play. He suggested they penalise him. What wonderful arrogance! He virtually said to them, 'Well, give me a two-stroke penalty and I'll play from there.' They knew he meant it too, so a compromise was struck and Nicklaus speeded up just a little!

Jack couldn't resist showing off his wonderful array of fruit trees. Like everything else in his life, they were perfect.

locks round the first finger of the left, simply known as 'interlocking', a grip that's seen something of a revival over the last ten to fifteen years. Tiger Woods is one of its devotees. By the age of fifteen Jack was winning local amateur titles both at junior and senior levels, and suddenly he was playing state and national golf. He won the Ohio Junior title and reached the semi-final of the US Junior Championships, first qualifying to play in the US Open when he was just seventeen.

By the end of the 1950s, while still in his teens, Nicklaus was one of the country's leading amateurs. He won the Amateur Championship in

Round about this time Arnold Palmer was at the height of his powers. He was the darling of the crowds, then along came Nicklaus and he started to beat their hero. They didn't like it at all. To them Jack was unsmiling, he didn't look the part, he was crumpled and rumpled, and although he walked quickly enough, he seemed to be over the ball for an age on every shot. Much was made of the early successes on the professional tour of Tiger Woods, but I can assure you, the impact Nicklaus made on the golfing scene was just as dramatic.

The first event he won as a professional, in 1962, was the US Open Championship. How about that

'It's the only tournament I've ever played in where I've wanted to finish second.' JACK NICKLAUS

AT THE 1997 US OPEN, COMPETING ALONGSIDE HIS SON GARY

for openers! From there successes flowed year after year after year. Even if you were to take the victories out of his CV and just concentrate on the number of times he finished in the top ten, those achievements would still make quite remarkable reading. Over the last year or two one of the main topics of conversation has been whether or not Tiger Woods will surpass the deeds of Nicklaus. Although Tiger has made an incredible start to his career, I wouldn't put a great deal of money on him outgolfing Nicklaus. Between 1962 and 1992 Jack won 70 tournaments on the Tour, 14 elsewhere in the world and 10 on the PGA Senior Tour, and as recently as 1998 finished tied for sixth in the Masters.

He and his wife Barbara have five children and umpteen grandchildren, and it would be fair to say that they dote on them all. They live in a delightful waterside family house in North Palm Beach, Florida, and have a fine motor cruiser/fishing boat tied up on a private jetty. Jack enjoys skiing, hunting and tennis; he has a grass court on his small estate that would cut the mustard at Wimbledon. There's a fine guest house too which, apart from being a very comfortable retreat for Jack's visitors, houses much of his hunting memorabilia. I remember staying there once when my wife was involved in a television cookery programme with Barbara Nicklaus. Jack wasn't going to take any part in the programme, but he couldn't resist showing off his wonderful array of fruit trees. Like everything else in his life they were perfect, a collection of the most magnificent grapefruit, avocado, orange and lemon trees you could ever hope to see.

One evening he decided to push the boat out and gave a drinks party. At some point I found myself in the guesthouse staring at the walls, adorned with all sorts of sporting trophies: huge fish the like of which I'd never seen before, and heads of moose and elk – dozens of them, an amazing sight, a taxidermist's dream. One thing, however, did put me off. By the side of the great fireplace – not that I imagine too many fires are ever lit in Florida – was the foot of an elephant which had been turned into a wastepaper basket. My thoughts were interrupted by a voice behind me uttering the immortal words, 'I guess Jack likes to kill things.' It took a couple of seconds for those words to sink in, and when I looked round the 'voice' had disappeared, but the sentiment stayed

with me for many years. For such a loving father to be so fascinated by 'killing things' is interesting. I wonder what Freud would have made of it.

How Jack has managed to fit in all his business activities alongside his golfing commitments is beyond me. His golf course architectural business is huge, and although some did not care for his early work, he has improved dramatically since, learning from past masters of the art and mixing their qualities with his own thoughts on how the game of golf should be played. However, he has been fortunate: in virtually every case he has had a huge budget to work with, which is a tremendous help. Try turning 125 acres of flat fields with a subsoil of galt clay and a client with little money into a great golf course. It's not a viable proposition. Some try it, but it's a lost cause.

Nicklaus performed so many incredible feats during his playing career that it's difficult to pick out specific moments when everything in his game clicked, but one tournament I shall always remember is the Masters in 1965. He started with a

67, which put him a couple of strokes behind the leader Gary Player, but after two rounds he was tied for the lead with Arnold Palmer and Player. He then went round in 64, a remarkable score, but it was the way the round was constructed that really caught my eye. He recorded eight birdies and ten pars, missed only a couple of fairways, and was on the green in the right number on every hole except the 17th, where his ball pitched on the green, spun back and ran off. He took 30 putts and no fives – yes, 30 putts. We hear drivel today, spoken by modern pros who say 'You can't make a living unless you *average* 28 putts a round' – it just shows you how poor their shots to the greens must be. The Augusta National has never been renowned for hard, bouncy conditions, and when you consider that the longest club Nicklaus used for any second shot was a three-iron, it shows how mightily he was striking the ball. After that round he was miles ahead of the field, and he stayed there, scoring a 69 on the final day to win by nine shots. The following year he won again to become the

'A guy went into a bar. He had his dog with him. He sat down and had a drink. All of a sudden the golf tournament came on TV and I was playing golf. I made a birdie and the dog did a flip on the bar. The next hole, I holed another putt and the dog did another flip. The bartender said, "This dog must really be a Nicklaus fan. What does he do when Nicklaus wins a tournament?" The guy said, "I don't know, I've only had him six years."'

JACK NICKLAUS
AT THE 1992 MASTERS

Left **Playing from one of Troon's bunkers, British Open, 1997 (© Popperfoto).**

In December 1998, *Sports Illustrated* named Jack Nicklaus top male individual athlete of the century, ahead of Muhammad Ali, Joe Louis, Sugar Ray Robinson, Rod Laver and Pete Sampras.

first man to defend the Masters title, but this time it was a much more closely fought affair. In fact, there was a three-way play-off over eighteen holes.

He had yet to win the British Open, though, and in 1966 he was coming over for a fifth attempt. There were many who thought Nicklaus might never master the art of seaside golf, for he hit the ball too high. That was fine when there was no wind, but how often did you play a championship course when there was no wind? He really must learn to play the 'Scottish run-up'. Still, Nicklaus was there or thereabouts every time our championship was played, and in 1966 he registered his first victory. That was the year Doug Sanders, runner-up to Jack along with Welshman Dave Thomas, uttered the immortal words when seeing the height of the rough, 'I don't want the first prize, just give me the hay concession.' And why not – I've never seen such terrifying rough in all my life. It was bordering on the ludicrous. The championship was a damned close-run thing, and with four holes left Nicklaus needed to finish in level par – three, five, four – to tie. He did better than that and squeezed home by a single stroke, suddenly alongside Hogan, Sarazen and Player as the only golfers to have won each of the four major championships. He would go on to complete that feat again, as if to emphasise, if that were necessary, his great superiority. And then, dammit, he did it again, three grand slams, a task completed in 1978 when the Open was played at St Andrews, a fitting venue.

After that, by his great standards there was a bit of a lull. People wondered whether they had seen the end of Nicklaus as a major force. But Jack went back to basics, going to see his original tutor, Jack Grout, and adding Phil Rodgers, a master of the short game, to his team of advisers. He started practising again. Why? He was 40, as rich as Croesus and acclaimed as the greatest player the world had ever seen. Surely it was a good time to relax? But it was reported that Nicklaus had said, 'My record isn't yet quite the one I want to leave behind', and although he didn't resuscitate his form at the drop of a hat, over the next few years he did some extraordinary things (mixed in with some diabolically untidy golf). He had succeeded in virtually reinventing himself. He'd lost 40lb in weight, let his hair grow, found a decent barber, and left Barbara to choose the clothes he would wear (primarily because Jack is colour-blind

and runs the risk of appearing in some very bizarre outfits).

There's no doubt he got a great thrill out of being hailed as the greatest golfer of all time, but he didn't suffer fools, not at all. Many a reporter in the press room at close of play has received a withering look from the cold, blue eyes of Nicklaus. Well, some do ask crass questions: 'Sixty-four today, Jack, did you hole any good putts?', 'Sixty-four, Jack, are you pleased with that?', and so on. But in his own way Jack was ever gracious.

He and Barbara are a wonderful team, and despite recent hip surgery and an ailing back Jack continues to play, continually saying that he will not become a ceremonial golfer – a slight dig at Arnold Palmer perhaps. But dammit, he is on the verge of becoming a ceremonial golfer. One wonders how much of that is due to his business commitments, the need to keep his name in the public eye, choosing where and when he plays in Senior events, trying to show well in the 'big ones'. What an amazing run he's had in those major events. He's played in around 150 consecutive major championships in Britain and the United States and won nineteen of them (21 if you count his two US Amateur Championships), and has 70 victories on the US Tour, but you still get the feeling that he wants to win.

For me, Jack Nicklaus is the master. Day in and day out he thought better than the rest. Yes, in his younger days he had great power, but so did other players; he was a wonderful striker of long irons, but there were others. There were departments of his game that weren't half as good as many, yet when you put the whole package together he became nigh on invincible. I've known Jack for over 40 years and in all that time I've never seen him throw away a tournament. I put that to him once. He thought for a moment, then came back with the classic answer, 'I guess I could keep playing my game when the rest of them could no longer keep playing theirs.' That just about sums up Jack Nicklaus' quality. He is the man with the most remarkable record in the world of golf. It's a record that may be beaten in the years ahead, but whatever path the world travels over the next hundred years the name of Jack Nicklaus will always be right at the top of the tree.

Left **Jack performed so many incredible feats that it's difficult to pick out specific moments** (© Popperfoto).

Pages 102 & 103 **Jack Nicklaus is the master. Day in and day out he thought better than the rest** (© Empics).

GREG NORMAN

FACT FILE

FULL NAME: Gregory John Norman

BORN: 10 February 1955;
Mt Isa, Queensland, Australia

TOURNAMENT WINS: 75
USA 18
Europe 14
Other 43

MAJORS: 2
Masters 0 (T2nd 1986; T2nd 1987; 2nd in 1996)
US Open 0 (2nd 1984; 1995)
The Open 2 (1986; 1993)
US PGA 0 (2nd 1986; 1993)

US MONEY LIST WINS: 3
1986; 1990; 1995

EUROPEAN ORDER OF MERIT WINS: 1
1982

HIGHEST WORLD RANKING: 1
11 times (total 331 weeks) 1986–98

PRESIDENTS CUP RECORD:
Appearances & Team Wins (W) 3 (1996–2000/1W)
Matches (Won-Lost-Halved) 14 (7–6–1)
Wins (Singles-Foursomes-Fourballs) 7 (1–2–4)

Above **The second of his two British Open victories, in 1993 (© Empics).**

Right **Greg Norman gives pleasure wherever he plays (© Empics).**

Pages 106 & 107 **Striding out at Sandwich, July 1993 (© Popperfoto).**

My first sighting of Greg Norman was in 1977 when he appeared in Great Britain under the watchful eye of Guy Wolstenholme, my old friend from years ago who had turned professional, emigrated to Australia and was given a brief to keep an eye on the young Queenslander as this was the first time he had been away from home. He was a relatively late starter, approaching his middle teens when he got the golfing bug, but it wasn't long before he was startling the world of golf with his ball striking and his keenness to do well.

He was introduced to me as one of the game's up-and-coming players at the Downfield Golf Club on the outskirts of Dundee, where the BBC were shooting an instructional golf series, and what a fine figure he struck with his blond hair and athletic build. You didn't have to be a genius to spot that this young man had some raw talent that, if harnessed correctly and allied to a half decent golfing brain, was going to go far.

So much has been written about Norman that it's hard to encapsulate it in just a few words. There's no doubt when you look at his victory record in the world's major golfing events that it's much too short. Oh, I agree, some of his mistakes at critical times were self-induced. Self-destruct is a term that has been used many times when describing Greg Norman – lack of fire, lack of fibre, a nervous streak – yet he has also been the recipient of some strokes of outrageous misfortune, and how often have I seen him win events in the real heat of battle when just getting the ball down the fairway has called for the greatest skill and nerve? He's won our Open Championship twice, but who will forget his demise on a number of occasions at Augusta, to which course his game is ideally suited? With one hand on the trophy, from the middle of the 18th fairway he blasted his second shot way to the right into the crowd, then fiddled about from there and a chance was gone. Larry Mize holed out from 40

yards at the second play-off hole when surely Norman must have felt he was in with a strong chance of victory. Not to mention that tragic last round with Nick Faldo in 1996.

And that's not all. He lost to Fuzzy Zoeller in a play-off for the US Open. Bob Tway, in the PGA Championship of 1986, holed a bunker shot on the final hole to win by a shot, though in terms of bad luck I suppose that wasn't too bad because Norman had been a number of strokes ahead with nine holes to play only for a few destructive shots to creep in. Still, you wouldn't have thought Tway would have been able to conjure up such an amazing shot just at that moment to steal victory.

But all these blows, which would have sunk a lesser man, were shrugged aside. There was no sign of complacency or complaint, it was just one of those things, and off he went to win other tournaments the length and breadth of the golfing world, giving pleasure wherever he went.

He has wide-ranging interests in the business world – golf-course design and development, agronomy, wine, boat building, clothing, you name it, Norman's involved in it, and he's successful too – but I wonder what will happen when he reaches 50 in February 2005. Will he do a Tom Watson, a Hale Irwin, a Palmer and Nicklaus and perform on the US Senior Tour? Will he wish to carry on displaying his skills, and effectively have a second career on the course? I think he may do if his levels of enjoyment are still reasonably high, but it wouldn't surprise me if he gave it all up and just played for fun.

He has been a breath of fresh air in the world of golf. It has been a delight to watch him play, and I still, perhaps misguidedly, think there may be one more round left in the breech. Oh, and wouldn't I be ever so joyful if he could win at Augusta and once and for all put that ignominious defeat at the hands of Nick Faldo behind him.

Greg Norman, truly a renaissance man.

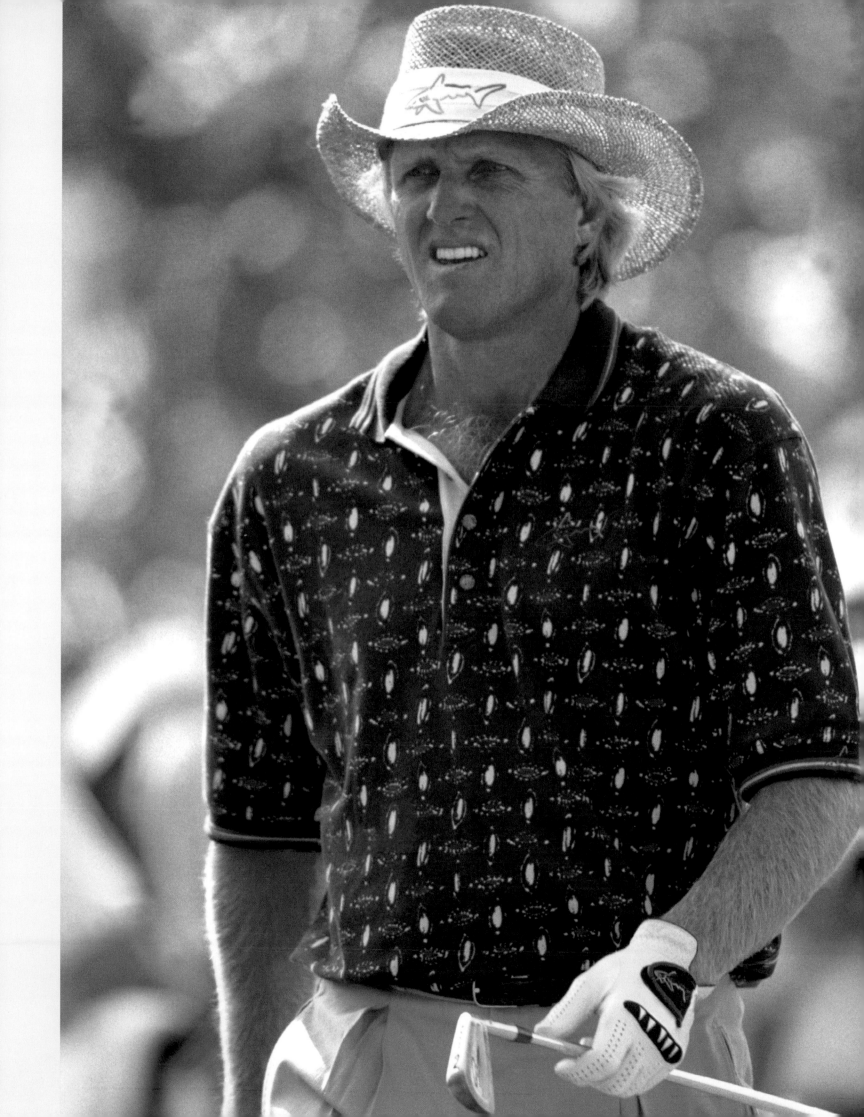

ARNOLD PALMER

FACT FILE

FULL NAME: Arnold Daniel Palmer

BORN: 10 September 1929; Latrobe, Pennsylvania, USA

TOURNAMENT WINS: 82
USA 60
Europe 7
Other 5
US Senior 10

MAJORS: 7 (8)
Masters 4 (1958; 1960; 1962 after play-off; 1964)
US Open 1 (1960)
The Open 2 (1961; 1962)
US PGA 0 (T2nd 1964; T2nd 1968; T2nd 1970)
US Amateur 1 (1954)
US Senior Open 1 (1981 after play-off)
PGA Seniors 2 (1980; 1984)

US MONEY LIST WINS: 4
1958; 1960; 1962; 1963
US Senior Tour 0
Highest: 4th 1980; 1981; 1982; 1984

RYDER CUP RECORD:
Appearances & Team Wins (W) 6 (1961–73/5W inc playing captain in 1963/1W); captain (non-playing) 1975 (1W)
Matches (Won-Lost-Halved) 32 (22–8–2)
Wins (Singles-Foursomes-Fourballs) 22 (6–9–7)

PRESIDENTS CUP RECORD:
Appearances & Team Wins (W); captain (non-playing) 1998 (1W)

Above **Winner of the Piccadilly World Matchplay tournament, October 1967 (© Empics).**

Right **Palmer has played a central role in the success of the US's Senior Tour (© Allsport).**

I first set eyes on Arnold Palmer in 1960 when he finished runner-up to Kel Nagle in the Centenary Open Championship at St Andrews. He came to Scotland with a big reputation and brought a whole new style of play to the world of golf. People who were old enough compared him to Walter Hagen, a 'go for broke' golfer. Palmer's motto was 'If I can hit it, I might hole it'. Keith McKenzie, the then Secretary of the Royal & Ancient Golf Club of St Andrews, was more than instrumental in getting Palmer – and, indeed, Jack Nicklaus – to come and compete in our Open Championship, which had lost some of its glitter. The Australian Kel Nagle, although a well-known and popular figure in the world of golf, wasn't really considered 'Open Championship material', but in spite of a very mixed bag of weather Nagle kept his nerve and emerged a worthy winner. However, a spark had been ignited in Palmer, who declared there and then that he would return and keep on returning until he had won the coveted claret jug.

His wait was short. He won flamboyantly the very next year at Royal Birkdale, and from then on became a very welcome visitor to these shores. He successfully defended his title the following year at Royal Troon. The course was burnt to a cinder by a long dry spell and drying winds, but he managed to keep the ball in play, putted beautifully and ran out a handsome winner.

Palmer came from a golfing family; his father worked at the Latrobe Golf Club on the outskirts of Pittsburgh. He was a good young player and was offered a scholarship at Wake Forest, one of the most prestigious American colleges. In 1954 he won the Amateur Championship, then did his National Service with the Coast Guard, and shortly afterwards turned professional. Although he wasn't a tall man, round about 5ft 10in, he had tremendously powerful arms and hands, and he was immediately successful, winning the Canadian Open Championship in 1955. That first year he

finished just outside the top 30 on the US Tour money list, and in both 1956 and 1957 he won four tournaments. Today these achievements would have reaped much gold and would certainly have put a player at the top of the money list, but that was not the case in those days. Believe it or not, he had not yet really found fame.

It was 1958 that saw him make that vital leap forward. He 'only' won three events that year, but one of them was the US Masters, during which, in all truth, he produced no great fireworks and two other players, Doug Ford and Fred Hawkins, missed opportunities on the final green to force a play-off. Still, Palmer had won his first professional major at the age of 28 – the age at which Bobby Jones retired – to become the youngest Masters champion for the best part of three decades.

If he helped elevate the British Open Championship to new levels, he certainly did the same for the Masters and the town of Augusta. This was where Arnie's armies began. They were noisy, cheering his every stroke, giving him enormous confidence but at the same time annoying some of his fellow competitors. But he went his merry way playing his own particular brand of golf, travelling the world and showing off his great skills. He was a key member, with Nicklaus and Player, of the 'big three'. At the time they were the modern triumvirate, to all intents and purposes personifying the world of professional golf. They toured Australia, Europe and South America and were signed up by the top golf-club and ball manufacturers of the day. All three were entirely different personalities and players, and all three attracted their own followers.

Rather like Hagen, Palmer's prowess and the things he did – and, occasionally, the things he was unable to do – made huge headlines. He won in spectacular fashion and lost equally dramatically. His victory in the US Open at Cherry Hills near Denver,

Colorado was quite remarkable. Palmer trailed Mike Souchak by seven strokes going into the final round, so obviously he was out of the picture. Still, during a quick lunch break before the final round he told an American journalist friend, Bob Drum, that he might still be in with a chance if he could shoot a spectacular round. Drum allegedly told him, 'You'll need at least a 65 to have any chance at all.'

He started off in fine style, the first hole a slightly downhill par four, just about driveable if you had a bit of a tail wind and the golfing gods on your side. Palmer gave his tee shot a mighty blow, reached the edge of the green, two-putted for a birdie three and off he went. The birdies flowed easily and quickly, he reached the turn in 30, came home in 35 and was the champion.

However, that spectacular victory was balanced by his remarkable collapse against Billy Casper in the 1966 US Open at the Olympic Country Club just outside San Francisco. With one round to go Palmer had a three-stroke lead and was paired on that final day with Casper. Palmer reached the turn in 32, seven strokes ahead, and it seemed to be all over. Some say Arnold's thoughts were on Ben Hogan's 1948 US Open aggregate record of 276, which he was set to break if he could get home in 36. With just four holes left it looked as if he would do it easily, even though he was a stroke over par for the back nine. Casper was still five strokes behind at this stage but, thanks to some sensible play from Casper and some ridiculous miscues from Palmer, the situation changed. Palmer began to spray shots all over the course and compounded those errors by endeavouring to bring off the most incredible recoveries. The crowd couldn't believe what they were watching. By the time the players reached the final hole they were all square. Palmer again found trouble from the tee and ended up having to sink a downhill five-footer on the last green to tie Casper. He holed it.

The next day there was an eighteen-hole play-off, and before long it once again looked as though Palmer would be the clear winner. He reached the turn in 33, two strokes ahead, but everything changed at the 12th. Both were in trouble with their tee shots, but Casper made the green in two and holed a long putt for a three while Palmer got to the green in three only a yard or so from the hole and missed. Then he took a seven at the par-five 16th and sadly it all went up in smoke.

Left **Arnie lets it rip off the tee at Turnberry, 1977** (© Empics).

Below **Palmer's motto was: 'If I can hit it, I might hole it'** (© Phil Sheldon).

How much that experience eroded Palmer's confidence is hard to say. He was still only 36, but he was never quite the same again. Although he occasionally won tournaments all around the world, the big ones eluded him. No longer was he able to strike those five- and six-footers into the back of the hole as if they were mere tap-ins. He'd never been afraid to tinker with his clubs or change his putter, but now he was collecting them by the dozen. Moreover, although golf was always the predominant way in which he made his living, his business activities were beginning virtually to override his golf. There was a time when it was said

that everything Arnold did made him money. Just think of all those endorsements, shoes, socks, trousers, shirts, sweaters, gloves, hats, umbrellas, food products, shaving creams, toiletries, dry-cleaning businesses, new car franchises and Cadillac agencies. I think there was even a line of Arnold Palmer loo paper!

It would be wrong, however, to say that after 1966 Palmer was a spent force. In 1971, for instance, he won four events and finished third in the money list. Things really started to disintegrate only from the mid- to late 1970s, although wherever he went he continued to be fêted. To some, though, including myself, it was an embarrassment to see the great man play poorly. He continually told anyone who would listen – and there were many listeners – that he loved the game, he came out to see his friends, they had supported him and as long as they wanted to come and watch him he would perform. It's hard to imagine that happening in any other form of business or entertainment, though. Would you really want to listen to singers, whether modern or classical, hitting the wrong note, or concert pianists doing no better on the ivories than Eric Morecambe or Les Dawson? For all that, the Arnold Palmer story is one of wonder and glory, flawed perhaps by the fact that the number of years during which he was winning major championships was far smaller than many of us thought it would be.

Until his later years – not only did he smoke but he enjoyed a cocktail or two – Palmer enjoyed very good health. He had married his childhood sweetheart, Winnie, and they had two daughters. I often wonder if, at the back of his mind, he was slightly disappointed not to have sired a son, but when I spoke to him at length on the subject many years later, in a funny way he was pleased because the young fella would have had to put up with constant comparisons. He gave a tremendous amount of his time to people, and I'm sure he never knowingly brushed aside an autograph seeker. Among some of the cynics, that became a bit of a joke. They would say things like 'Arnold's in the car park looking for someone to give an autograph to' – unkind, particularly when you compare it to the brusqueness, bordering on rudeness, of many of the good players over the last 25 years. It can be a pain to stop and sign

Above **Arnie's army is out in force at the 1971 Ryder Cup** (© Popperfoto).

He flew around the world setting records for private flights. He used his plane at every opportunity, and when he wasn't using it he rented it out. Arnold always knew the value of money. Very little, if any, of his vast fortune was squandered.

He became one of the few professional golfers to be made an Honorary Member of the Royal & Ancient Golf Club of St Andrews. He's also a full member at Augusta. Many people are under the false impression that when a player wins the Masters and dons his green blazer he's automatically a member of the club. Not so. Former champions can't just arrive with a few friends and play whenever they feel like it, although they can 'get on to the course' if they go through the proper channels, but only on a limited number of occasions during the year. A full membership, however, is an entirely different kettle of fish, although the course is only open for a maximum of seven months a year due to the weather conditions that prevail.

Like Walter Hagen and Henry Cotton, Arnold Palmer changed the face of golf and the attitudes of those in high places towards professional golfers. When he first began his life on the US Tour the total prize money in all events amounted to less than a million dollars. For 2002 an astonishing $198 million is up for grabs. There are also several minor tours going on around the world where young professionals can learn their trade, hoping to be promoted to the premier division. Then there's the Senior Tour, in whose enormous success Palmer played a central role.

Many of us have enjoyed the skills and precision of Ben Hogan, the beautiful rhythm and elegant walk of Sam Snead, but Palmer brought excitement to golf. TV ratings soared. It's impossible to summarise all he has done in and for the game. For a long period he was the most exciting player I've ever seen. Not only that, he was fun to be with.

autographs, particularly when you're on an urgent errand; sometimes it's hard to explain to those waiting in line that you really must go. They, in turn, can feel slighted, and for ever more they'll curse the name of the person who didn't have time to sign. But from the early days Palmer was loved, and in later years, when he hardly featured on any leaderboard, he was adored – not at all like those who are greatly admired but never loved, let alone adored.

One of his great passions was flying, and as soon as he could afford it he bought himself a relatively modest plane, quickly graduating to executive jets.

Below **Yet another putt reaches its target, October 1964 (© Empics).**

Pages 114 & 115 **Expertly splashing out of one of Wentworth's sand traps, 1971 (© Empics).**

GARY PLAYER

Above **Player won the British
Open in the 1950s, the 1960s
and the 1970s. Here he has the
1974 claret jug** (© Popperfoto).

Right **Gary says his black clothes
help to keep the heat in and give
him more power** (© Empics).

If I had to pick two supreme champions where dedication, tenacity, drive, guts and spirit were the main criteria, two people would come to mind: Ben Hogan and Gary Player. There have been many hard workers in the game of golf, but surely none worked harder than Hogan and Player and received just rewards for their efforts.

I first saw Gary Player in the early 1950s. Just 5ft 7in tall and slight of build, his talent looked very limited. He spent hours hitting balls with the most unelegant swing – there was no rhythmical flow to it at all – his chipping style was not much better, and although he did have the ability to play bunker shots reasonably well, his putting stroke was just a jab. For the life of me I couldn't see him going anywhere. I remember watching him, with John Jacobs, practising an impossible chip shot at Crans sur Sierre, that magical golfing/skiing venue high in the Alps. He was pitching on to a downhill slope, ground like concrete, trying to get the ball to stop within 25 feet, a total impossibility. We watched spellbound; had the lad lost his reason? We moved closer, he turned to asked for advice. If memory serves me right, in the nicest possible way we suggested he return to South Africa, enjoy golf as an amateur and get a steady job that might include a pension.

Gary Player was the third child of Harry Player, who worked as a foreman in the gold mines and played to a handicap of two. Gary's mother died when he was only eight and his older brother, Ian, eight years his senior, was to be a great influence on his rather weak sibling, teaching him to box, climb, ride and participate in all aspects of physical endeavour. He made huge strides in golf between the ages of twelve and eighteen. In 1953, when he was eighteen, he turned professional, and in his first year, on the rather limited South African Tour, he registered one second-place finish and finished the season ranked in the top dozen. In 1954 he won his first tournament, the East Rand Open.

Bobby Locke was the great South African player of the day, and in many ways he encouraged the youngster. Soon Player had won a second tournament, the Egyptian Matchplay Championship at the Gezira Club just outside Cairo where John Jacobs was the professional. It didn't cause much of a stir, but in those far-off days the event attracted a goodly field and winning was important, particularly for a young player. Despite his shortcomings he went from strength to strength. In 1956 he won the 90-hole Dunlop Tournament over the New Course at Sunningdale, then made a big decision to try the US Tour (remember, at that time it took 46 hours to fly from Johannesburg to America). It paid off: in 1958 he won the Kentucky Open and finished second in the US Open Championship to Tommy Bolt, and then, lo and behold, at Muirfield in 1959 Player won the Open. Perhaps we shouldn't have been so surprised because in 1956 he'd come fourth, and he'd finished seventh in 1958.

What drama unfolded on that final day at Muirfield! Player was four behind with one round to go, only hanging on by the skin of his teeth because he'd played the last nine of the third round in 33. The afternoon round began well – he was out in 34 and had three more birdies – and he arrived at the last hole, a wonderful par four back to the clubhouse, requiring a four for a 66 and a total of 282 which surely would be good enough. But he put his tee shot in the bunker, could only reach the green in three, and then three-putted for a two-over-par six. He was just 23 years old and very emotional. Vivienne, his wife, tried to console him, but he would have none of it. He felt his chance had gone, that perhaps another would never come along. Yet all was not lost. After all, a 68 was still a wonderful score and those players to come had to score in the low 70s to catch him. One by one they fell by the wayside; one club professional, Fred Bullock – whose daughter

I remember watching him practising pitching on to a downhill slope, ground like concrete, trying to get the ball to stop within 25 feet. In the nicest possible way we suggested he return to South Africa, enjoy golf as an amateur and get a steady job that might include a pension.

Above **Shaking hands with Jack Nicklaus at the World Matchplay Championship, 1966** (© Empics).

Left **Searching for his ball in the pond at Augusta's 15th hole, 1974** (© Popperfoto).

pulled one of those newfangled trolleys round the course as he couldn't afford a caddie – chased him home and was perhaps unfortunate not to have tied. I wonder where his life would have gone had he won. But it wasn't to be, and Player was on his way to becoming one of the leading figures in world golf.

An interesting point about Player's remarkable career is that many of his majors were won because his main challengers stumbled, if not fell, at the final hurdle. I'm sure he would have none of it, but let's just examine the evidence. In a play-off for the US Open with Australian Kel Nagle, it was nip and tuck with a few holes to go. Nagle, one of the straightest hitters in golf, pulled his tee shot into trouble, hit a woman spectator on the head and laid her low. Blood was pumping everywhere, although in the end it turned out to be only a flesh

wound. A sensitive soul, the Australian was very upset by this, and Player went on to win.

When he came home in 30 to win one of his Masters titles, Hubert Green, one of the best putters the world has ever seen, had a three-and-a-half-footer downhill to tie, but he was disturbed as he bent over to putt. Was it the TV commentary or a radio reporter? Who knows? He stopped, backed away and missed. The Masters saw another remarkable happening for Player. Arnold Palmer arrived on the final tee with a four to win and a five to tie. After a decent drive, he pushed his second shot into the right-hand bunker. From there, a thinned shot over the green flew into the crowd, he was forced to pitch back, and missed the putt. The great man, at the height of his fame, had taken a six at the final hole at Augusta to hand the title to the South African.

He's had his fortunate moments, too. In the US PGA Championship, coming towards the end of the final round, Player pushed his tee shot into what looked like impenetrable grass. He had a shot of well over 100 yards to reach the flag, and there were trees and water in the way. He smashed it with every sinew in his body, the ball came out clean and true, flew over the trees and finished within a few feet of the hole. He kept his nerve, holed the putt, and became the PGA champion.

At the British Open Championship played at Royal Lytham & St Annes, Player, very much in control, hooked his second shot to the left of the 17th green into a patch of rough about the size of a tennis court. He and his caddie, 'Rabbit' Dyer, looked and looked and looked, but there was no sign of it. Dyer was frantic, time was running out. How quickly the allotted four minutes can disappear when there's an air of panic, but with seconds left a cry rang out, 'Here it is!' Player managed to hack it out, and got a five, but the drama wasn't over yet. He put his second shot through the back of the green at the 18th, up against the clubhouse, and had to revert to putting with the back of his putter to scuttle the ball back on to the green. That he did, and two putts later, despite this ragged finish, he was the champion. Some scurrilous stories circulated afterwards that the following day a search party had gone out to the 17th and, depending on which story you heard, found a ball or several balls with the same number on. I'm sure Player must have heard these wicked

Above **Enjoying a successful putt, October 1974 (© Empics).**

Right **Driving off during the 2001 British Open (© Empics).**

Pages 122 & 123 **Practice makes perfect. An expertly played bunker shot, October 1971 (© Empics).**

stories but, as with a lot of things that have happened in his golfing life, they sailed serenely over his head.

He can, on occasion, be rather hypocritical. He pontificates long and hard on many things and sometimes presents a holier-than-thou image. He's continually thanking 'someone' for the fact that he's still hale and hearty, and there's no doubt he will win a golf tournament somewhere in the seventh decade of his life. If he sticks to his fruit and nut diet and 400 press-ups a day, he should live to be 120. Many of us have heard these stories time and time again, yet there's something about

him that makes us forgive his verbal extravagances. Dammit, he's done it all, much against the odds, forever David pitted against Goliath. His record in the World Matchplay Championship at Wentworth, played every year in October, is quite remarkable. But again, he's blessed with the ability to 'niggle', something that's easily done in matchplay but never really occurs in medal play.

He's earned and spent fortunes, mostly on family and hobbies. At an early age he became interested in livestock and started breeding quarter horses, soon graduating to thoroughbreds. Indeed, he had a runner in the Derby several years ago. He has a glorious estate outside Johannesburg called Blair Atholl, a name taken from the estate of the Duke of Buccleuch. He also runs a school for young blacks on his estate. When I visited him there were at least 60 or 70 youngsters there, all seemingly as happy as Larry. He provides transport to bring them in each morning and take them home, teachers' fees, food, beverage, the lot.

He and Vivienne produced at least five or six children. The boys tried their hand at golf but they couldn't get anywhere near father's great deeds, although they are involved with him in his very successful golf course design company. Like Arnold Palmer, Jack Nicklaus, Byron Nelson and Ben Hogan, Player is blessed with a wonderful wife. Although his background was a relatively poor one, the pair of them have kept their feet firmly on the ground.

His record is remarkable, both on the main and the Senior Tour. He continues to travel, and, over and above his golfing prowess, he will be remembered for many things. Those outrageous black and white trousers he wore at St Andrews in an early Open Championship, for instance, one leg white, one leg black. He became the Black Knight, playing even on the hottest day dressed entirely in funereal colours (he said it helped to keep the heat in and gave him more power!). He avoided white bread, potatoes, fried food, sugar, rich food in general, and extolled the virtues of wheatgerm, vegetable juices, oats, nuts, dried fruit, fresh fruit, fish. His body was and is a temple. 'The more I practise, the luckier I get' was one of his quotes, but the one I like the best is this: 'You should look after your body. If you do, it could last a lifetime.' Gary, I love you.

'You should look after your body.
If you do, it could last you a lifetime.'
GARY PLAYER

NICK PRICE

FACT FILE

FULL NAME: Nicholas Raymond Leige Price

BORN: 28 January 1957; Durban, South Africa

TOURNAMENT WINS: 39
USA 17
Europe 5
Other 17

MAJORS: 3
Masters 0 (5th 1986)
US Open 0 (T4th 1992; 4th 1998)
The Open 1 (1994)
US PGA 2 (1992; 1994)

US MONEY LIST WINS: 2
1993; 1994

EUROPEAN ORDER OF MERIT WINS: 0
Highest: 14th 1980

HIGHEST WORLD RANKING: 1
Once (43 consecutive weeks) 1994–95

PRESIDENTS CUP RECORD:
Appearances & Team Wins (W) 4 (1994–2000/1W)
Matches (Won-Lost-Halved) 19 (7–8–4)
Wins (Singles-Foursomes-Fourballs) 7 (1–4–2)

Above **Nick Price has one of the simplest swings in the world of professional golf (© Popperfoto).**

Right **Teeing off at Medinah's 9th hole during the 1999 PGA Championship (© Popperfoto).**

There's an old saying in sport that nice guys finish second. Nick Price is one of the very few who can bury that old cliché. That's not to say that underneath that gentle demeanour is anything other than a character as tough as old boots, but he has a wonderful ability to smile, to spare time for people and, even under the most strained circumstances, be courteous.

Price has one of the simplest swings in the world of professional golf, although one might say he has a little 'twirly bit' at the top of the backswing and his rhythm is quick. His balance, though, is impeccable, his crispness of strike most impressive. I suppose the one thing over the years that hasn't reached the high standards of other departments of his game has been his putting, but when you consider what a majestic striker of the ball he is and how many times he puts himself within holing range, you realise that because he has so many opportunities to make birdies he also has more opportunities to miss! At the opposite end of the scale you get players who are, in a way, erratic with their shots to the green but have a magical short game, able to chip and one-putt, sometimes from the most outrageous situations, much to the chagrin of their opponents. Seve Ballesteros was a prime example of this.

Price is one of the finest drivers I've ever seen, long enough, even in modern company, to hold his own. He had a wonderful run in the 1990s, including that very satisfying win at Turnberry over Jesper Parnevik, and it wouldn't be wrong to say that he was robbed of victory in the Open Championship at Royal Lytham & St Annes in 1988 when Seve won. Having started the final day with a two-stroke lead, he circumnavigated the course in 68, only to lose by a stroke to Seve, who went round in a flamboyant 65.

Originally Price's family came from England, but Nick was born in Durban, South Africa, on 28 January 1957. The family returned to England when great political changes took place in Africa. Northern and Southern Rhodesia became Zambia and Zimbabwe, along with many other countries whose first task when gaining independence was to change the name of the country and start up an airline! I'm sure Price still has many associations with and affection for his homeland, but home for the past few years has been in Florida.

Price still regularly competes and can, when the putter is behaving, put some wonderful scores together. One of the things that has always intrigued me are the chances he's taken with manufacturers. Several times over the last few years he's emerged advertising a new golf ball or golf clubs very few people have ever heard of. One can only assume it's done for business reasons, that the 'up front' money was substantial. In some cases those marriages have been successful, but occasionally his business 'friendships' have been put under severe strain.

It has always fascinated me how and why some players chop and change their equipment. Of course, the lure of big money is always there and it's very attractive, but if you're already using equipment you're really happy with and you're playing at the top of your form, you can surely win more money and get extra bonuses with them rather than going off on a tangent and not performing as well with clubs that suddenly don't 'perform'. This problem has manifested itself many times over the years, particularly with players like Gary Player, Nick Faldo and Ian Woosnam. Nick Price, on occasion, has not been far behind them.

Still, it has been a privilege to watch him progress over the years, to be in his company, and to marvel at his patience and friendliness, even though on occasion, I'm sure, he's muttered something under his breath that might not have been construed as being quite up to the wondrous image of Nick Price. A good fellow, a first-class professional and a huge asset to the game of golf.

GENE SARAZEN

Above **From the early 1920s until his death in 1999, Sarazen's fame never decreased (© Allsport).**

Right **Sarazen's name will be uttered whenever people gather and talk of golf and the game's great deeds (© Allsport).**

Born Eugenio Saraceni in Harrison, New York, Sarazen (as he later called himself) was largely self-taught and in some ways rather unorthodox. He stood only 5ft 5in tall but he had very strong hands and arms and a powerful pair of legs. He had a crude grip but it was good enough for him to be able to control the club head through the ball. I swear, if he'd had seven knuckles on his left hand, he would have shown them all.

His father, Federico, was a carpenter and had rather grand ideas. He would have liked to have gone into the priesthood, but that was impossible. Although his education was limited, Federico spoke polished Italian and much of his reading was in the classics, but he never managed to speak other than very heavily accented English. Apparently there was very little warmth between father and son. Sadly, as the years went by they grew further apart. Federico wanted his son to join him in the world of woodwork, but Eugene had other ideas.

He started caddying when he was about nine, and golf certainly introduced him to a much wider world. To supplement his income he sold newspapers and picked up scrap metal, and in the summer he'd go fruit picking. For a while he even had a job lighting the street gas lamps. While he was in his teens he contracted pneumonia and was not expected to live, but after a long struggle he recovered and decided to get himself a job in the open air. At the age of seventeen, by which time he was playing reasonable golf, he was apprenticed to one of the local professionals at the princely sum of eight dollars a week. Over the winter he would take himself off to Florida to work in one of the large railway yards. There were a few small local tournaments to be played in at this time, and he was relatively successful. Then a chance meeting led to him being offered a job as the assistant pro at the Fort Wayne Country Club in Indiana. His mother, Adela, was overjoyed. Federico, however,

was not pleased. He just couldn't believe his son could make a living in the world of golf, but at the age of nineteen Eugene landed his first full pro's job in Titusville and at the same time changed his name to Gene Sarazen.

It wasn't long before he moved on to Pittsburgh, and in 1922 he won the Southern Open. To the rank-and-file golfers, though, he was still an unknown when he arrived to play in the US Open at Skokie in Illinois. He began with rounds of 72 and 73 which put him right up with the leaders, but in the third round things were slightly different. He took 40 on the outward nine and came home in 35, but his score of 75 didn't put him completely out of touch. In fact, he was only four behind the leaders, who included Bobby Jones and Walter Hagen. In the final round Sarazen reached the turn in 33, dropped a shot at the tenth and parred his way in until the 18th, a par five of just under 500 yards straight into the wind. Sarazen hit two wonderful shots on to the green and two-putted for a round of 68, a very low score indeed for the early 1920s. Players didn't go out according to their scores in those far-off days, and Gene was one of the early starters, so he had set a very good target. As the day drew on it became more and more obvious that no one would catch him, and he ended the champion by just one shot from John Black, a virtually unknown 43-year-old, and Bobby Jones, who had yet to win his first US Open. Sarazen was just twenty years of age.

Although he wasn't the youngest man ever to win the US Open, he went on to become the youngest player ever to win the US PGA Championship a few months later, beating Walter Hagen, the greatest match player of the day, in a final which was written up at the time as a classic battle, going into extra holes.

Suddenly, Sarazen was elevated to the upper echelons of golfing royalty. Hagen, Jones and

Sarazen – perhaps the first Americans to be called the 'big three'. He came over and attempted to win the British Open, but it was not to be. Links golf was something entirely foreign to him – hard, bouncy ground, big, deep bunkers, wind at 20 to 30mph. Life there was hard, but in a masochistic way he enjoyed it and he promised himself he would return and at all costs win the British Open championship.

After this glorious start to his career, the next four years were miserable. He won only one tournament, chopped and changed his grip and style, tried to hit a higher trajectory. It was all such a struggle. Why had it been so easy in 1922? Perhaps because then he hadn't realised how difficult the game could be. Rather like José María Olázabal, driving was his Achilles heel, and on many occasions he used a three-wood from the tee, which helped him to be more accurate. The change in his fortunes came in 1927. He began to win three or four tournaments a year, but major

championships eluded him. He played quite well in the Open at Royal St George's in 1928 but was rather impetuous going for broke whenever the green was within reach, having not yet learnt when to attack and when to defend. But he relished the challenge of links golf and was still determined that one day he would win the Open.

By 1932, at the age of 30, his game was much more consistent. It was round about this time that Sarazen had a brainwave. Bunker play was a very hazardous business in those days. You could either use a thin-bladed lofted club, about the equivalent of a nine-iron today, and attempt to flick it clean off the top of the sand, or smash into the ground as hard as you could and hope for the best. Sarazen wanted a club with which he could hit behind the ball, follow through and take enough sand to propel the ball up and out under some form of control. Such a club did not exist, so Sarazen decided to invent one. He began by soldering lead on to the back flange of an old lofted club, and after much trial and error he produced a forerunner of today's modern sand iron. The club was legal, he became much more confident, and as a result he reckoned that more often than not he got down in two from greenside bunkers.

In 1933 the venue for the Open was Prince's near Sandwich in Kent, one of the three courses, along with Royal Cinque Ports and Royal St George's, whose boundaries virtually touch each other. Prince's was a long course, almost 7,000 yards, a formidable test when you think of the quality of the equipment available then. This was one of a number of championships in which my father, Percy Alliss, figured prominently; after a couple of rounds he was well in the hunt, just three behind the leader. Sarazen played quite brilliantly at times, although there were a few hiccups along the way. His final round was 74, but still he won by five strokes from Arthur Havers, the champion in 1923. His aggregate score of 283 beat the 285 set by Bobby Jones at St Andrews in 1927, and the record stood until 1950. My father always thought 1933 one of his best opportunities to win the championship, but he finished nine strokes behind having three-putted 23 times over the four rounds. He and Sarazen became good friends and played against each other a few times in Ryder Cup matches, and in the first US v. GB Seniors Matchplay event in the mid-1950s.

Below **Driving was Sarazen's Achilles heel** (© Allsport).

Sarazen had a crude grip but it was good enough for him to be able to control the club head through the ball. I swear, if he'd had seven knuckles on his left hand, he would have shown them all.

Right **Sarazen and Max Faulkner on Troon's 18th green, 1973** (© Popperfoto).

Sarazen, in all truth, wasn't playing particularly well either, but, like Gary Player, he always kept trying, hoping for a miracle. One happened. Sarazen's drive at the 485-yard 15th was a beauty, but the second shot was a formidable one: the flag was at the back of the green about 220 yards away, and there was a pond in front. Gene took out his trusty four-wood, turned the nose in a little bit and hit it with everything he had – rather reminiscent of a shot I played many years later at the 18th hole when partnering Christy O'Connor against Arnold Palmer and Dave Marr in a Ryder Cup fourball match at Royal Birkdale (but that's another story). Sarazen's ball carried over the water, ran on and on and into the hole for an albatross. He played out the remainder of the round in par and tied with Wood, winning the 36-hole play-off the next day by five shots. It was his seventh and last major championship victory.

I was fortunate enough to meet Gene Sarazen on many occasions. In fact, we were paired together for the first two rounds of the Open Championship at Royal Lytham & St Annes in 1952. He was then 50 years of age and, in all truth, played with a cavalier style which I thought at the time very off-putting. But I relished his charm, joviality and enthusiasm. Perhaps he doesn't rank quite as highly as some in this book, but he's here for two very good reasons: for inventing the forerunner of the sand iron, and for becoming one of the few people to achieve a professional Grand Slam – the Open Championships of the United States and Great Britain, the US PGA and the Masters. A wonderful achievement.

Over the years his fame never decreased. He appeared at the Masters every year in his familiar plus-fours, carrying his leather-seated shooting stick. His name and face live on in the constantly repeated *Shell's Wonderful World of Golf* TV series, which he co-hosted. What's so interesting now, watching those matches (in which I was privileged to play several times), is the poor condition of the golf courses and the sketchy camerawork, but then there were probably no more than three or four cameras deployed, and the commentary was stilted, particularly dear Gene's efforts. Although he did so much in the media, he was never comfortable in that capacity. Never mind, his name will be uttered whenever people gather and talk of golf and the game's great deeds.

Above **I relished Sarazen's charm, joviality and enthusiasm** (© Allsport).

Right **Not bad for a 71-year-old! Sarazen at the British Open, 1973** (© Popperfoto).

In the mid-1930s the Augusta National Golf Course opened, and in its second year Sarazen was the champion, but what drama unfolded on the 15th! Craig Wood was out early, and everyone agreed he was going to be the winner. Hagen, who had been well in the hunt, had faded and finished well down the field with a last round of 79.

SAM SNEAD

FACT FILE

FULL NAME: Samuel Jackson Snead

BORN/DIED:
b 27 May 1912; Hot Springs, Virginia, USA
d 23 May 2002; Hot Springs, Virginia, USA

TOURNAMENT WINS: 92
USA 81
Europe 1
Other 10

MAJORS:
Masters 3 (1949; 1952; 1954 after play-off)
US Open 0 (2nd 1937; 1947; 1949; 1953)
The Open 1 (1946)
US PGA 3 (1942; 1949; 1951)
 PGA Seniors 6 (1964; 1965; 1967; 1970; 1972; 1973)

US MONEY LIST WINS: 3
1938; 1949; 1950

RYDER CUP RECORD:
Appearances & Team Wins (W) 7 (1937–59/7W inc
playing captain 1951; 1959); captain (non-playing)
1969 (0W)
Matches (Won-Lost-Halved) 13 (10–2–1)
Wins (Singles-Foursomes) 10 (6–4)

Above **Snead could well qualify as the athlete of the century** (© Phil Sheldon).

Right **Practice day before the 1949 Ryder Cup** (© Popperfoto).

If anyone ever played golf in a more elegant way than Sam, I'd like to know who it was. He had everything: rhythm, balance, power, touch, skill, the most wonderful walk (almost rivalling that of Sean Connery) and a wicked sense of humour, even if at times it might have been considered rather 'bawdy'.

The year 1912 was a spectacular one for the world of golf, for it was the year in which three of the world's all-time greats were born. Nelson, Hogan and Snead – what a vintage Premier Cru indeed! None of them came from a 'privileged' background; in fact, Snead hailed from a tiny village called Ashwood in the foothills of West Virginia. He was the fifth son of Harry Snead, a man of Dutch/German extraction, and Laura, who was 47 at the time of his birth. That would surely have made the *Guinness Book of Records* had it been around at that time! Harry had a job maintaining the boilers at a local hotel and owned a smallholding where he kept a few cows and some chickens, which helped a lot during those impoverished years between the wars. Snead managed to enjoy a wonderful youth, roaming the hills, learning to trap and shoot, and keeping clear of the illegal liquor manufacturers, or 'moonshiners', who were rather apt to shoot at anything that moved.

He got the golfing bug by watching his brother, Homer, twelve years his senior, swinging a club down in the cow pasture, but Homer was no real help and didn't encourage Sam in any way – strange, that. His first couple of clubs were crude, homemade affairs with which he used to hit stones, acorns, anything that was small and spherical. He had some schooling and was an outstanding athlete, but eventually he decided to concentrate on golf, rather in the way Walter Hagen had done some years before. It was an individualistic sport, and that appealed to Snead. He began to do a bit of caddying, but was forced to

give it up when he got frostbite – shoes were only for school days and Sunday churchgoing!

He turned professional in 1934, aged 22. He wasn't on any sort of wage, but he could keep what he earned giving lessons. Then he had an amazing stroke of good luck: the golf manager at the Greenbrier Hotel in White Sulphur Springs saw Snead, was impressed, and offered him an assistant's job with a living wage. Now, the Greenbrier was a very smart establishment, and it was here that Snead was able to develop his game and begin to play competitive golf. In 1936 he won the West Virginia Championship, scoring a 61 in one round, which many thought at the time was a world record. He matched himself against visiting professionals and, watching them, was even more determined to go to tournaments and discover just what the golfing world was all about.

He found himself in Hershey, Pennsylvania, famous for its chocolate bars. He had no intention of playing, but, just in case, he took his clubs – nine in total and all odd, though to Snead they were wondrous. There he was, hanging around the 1st tee, when he was invited to join a practice round. He didn't make a very good start. His first three tee shots went out of bounds, but then he put the next one on the green, a drive of over 300 yards. Impatience and embarrassment suddenly changed to amazement. He scored reasonably well in the rest of the round and made up his mind to play in the tournament. Having aired his decision, no one objected – far different from the sophisticated process of today. He finished fifth and won a few bucks, but more importantly his confidence suddenly sprouted wings and he decided to try the Tour.

Prize money was very small in the mid-1930s; you had to finish in the top half dozen to cover your expenses, but still Sam gave it a go. The first couple of events were not encouraging and he

'He would do 50 one-arm push-ups with me sitting on his back.' SAM'S SON, JACK, EXPLAINS HIS FATHER'S FITNESS REGIME

'Cheapest I'll play for is $25 Nassau. Any less than that, I'd rather sit home and watch the squirrels.'

SAM SNEAD

began to wonder if, after all, he'd made the right choice. It was in Oakland in the sunny state of Florida that Snead finally struck oil. His four rounds, 69, 65, 69 and a final 67, brought him $1,200 in prize money. He stole all the headlines, and would continue to do so for more than 50 years. The press loved him and so did the spectators for, apart from his wonderful, relaxed style and easy elegance, he hit the ball amazing distances with the most exquisitely balanced swing, quickly earning the nickname 'Slamming Sam'. I don't think he was altogether happy with this in later life because it rather implied that all he could do was hit the ball hard.

One of the other reasons the press took him so much to heart was the fact that he came from 'the wrong side of the tracks'. It was rather romantic to think that Sam Snead, a hillbilly with no experience of the outside world, should suddenly reach the top of the tree so quickly, and apparently without much effort. His naivety produced a host of stories, some of them apocryphal but most of them amusing. When Snead was shown a picture of himself in the *New York Times* after his win in Oakland, he gasped, 'How on earth did they get that? I ain't never been to New York in my life.' He was fortunate that Fred Corcoran, the Mark McCormack of the day, spotted his potential and made himself Snead's manager with the words, 'No Hollywood script writer could have invented Sam Snead, he's the real article.' He had all the magic ingredients promoters dream about, and early on found his famous trademark: a straw hat with a colourful band, which he always wore at a jaunty angle.

The Bing Crosby Tournament on the Monterey peninsular was something special. All the best players wanted to compete alongside Bing's famous friends from the world of entertainment and business. Snead won in fine style, but then he went into a bit of a slump. He'd been written up as

a mighty hitter, and now he went through a period where that was all he tried to do. He wanted to hear the ooohs and aaahs of the crowd as he smote the ball away into the distance, and it didn't help his cause when promoters and organisers always seemed to pair him with other big hitters – Lawson Little and Jimmy Thompson come immediately to mind. Although Sam *was* a big hitter, he could be unreliable, especially when he was really letting everything go. The problem was his driver, which was much too light and whippy, but generous fellow professional Henry Picard gave him a driver with a much stiffer shaft weighing about fourteen and a half ounces. After just a few hits Snead fell head over heels in love with his new toy and stayed faithful to it for many years.

His form almost immediately returned, so much so that when the US Open came round in 1937 he was favourite – yes, favourite, despite the fact that he had competed in only seven tournaments as a professional. He didn't disappoint the crowd, opening with a 69 for a share of the lead and following that with a 73 and a 70, which left him just one stroke behind Ed Dudley and level with Ralph Guldahl. Snead's finish was dramatic to say the least. A long way from the green on the final hole, he hit a three-wood to within a couple of yards or so. The putt went in for an eagle three and the crowds were ecstatic.

Once inside the safety of the clubhouse the press overpowered him and all sorts of people were waving contracts. Then news came from out on the course that Guldahl had only to par his remaining holes to equal Snead's total of 283. The gods were not on Sam's side. Guldahl holed a couple of good putts and a monster for an eagle three to win by two. I'm sure that had Snead won the championship that year he would have gone on to win at least three or four more. It was a great disappointment, but everyone, including Sam, thought his time was bound to come. After all,

Right **Snead died in May 2002, just short of his ninetieth birthday. He was a remarkable talent** (© Phil Sheldon).

Below **Making his acceptance speech after winning the Teachers World Seniors Championship at Wentworth, 1964** (© Phil Sheldon).

Ralph Guldahl had defended his championship, and, dammit, Snead was a far better player.

Snead challenged again in 1939. He was leading after the first two rounds with scores of 68 and 71, but slipped up a bit in the third, four-putting one green. Even so, a 73 put him just one stroke off the lead, and he set off for the final round full of confidence. Those four putts were surely just an aberration; he'd putted very well in those early years. With just a couple of holes left to play it looked as if he was certain to break 70. As it turned out, a 69 would have tied Guldahl's 1937 US Open record score of 281 and given Snead a three-stroke victory, but it wasn't to be. On the 17th he missed a short putt and bogeyed the hole, but still, coming up the last, he needed only to par to beat the best score in, Byron Nelson's 284.

The 18th measured 550 yards, a very strong par five. Snead felt he had to birdie the hole. Unfortunately there was a long wait while the spectators were cleared off the fairway. Whether this distracted him or not shall never be known; what is known is that he hooked his tee shot into trampled rough some 260 yards from the green with bunkers to carry. The sensible shot would have been to play out short with a middle iron and then pitch up, but Sam had it in his head that he needed a birdie for victory (remember, this was over 60 years ago and there were no scoreboards dotted around the course). He decided he'd have to go for it with his second, but he didn't catch it well and it found a slightly buried lie in a fairway bunker. There were still 100 yards or more to go, and the bunker face was very close. Again Sam spurned safety. A sand iron just up and out was the shot, but, no, he thought he could reach the green with an eight-iron. He caught the ball thin, it jammed in the face of the bunker, and a few minutes later Snead was left with a putt of ten to twelve yards for a six to tie Nelson. He took three for the most famous eight in US Open history – at least until Tze Chung Chen took eight at the 5th hole during the final round at Oakland Hills in 1985.

In the space of three years Snead had let the championship slip through his fingers twice, once through a Jean van der Velde type of mistake, the other because of a brilliant last round from the eventual winner, but again, time was surely on his side. But it wasn't. He had another chance in 1940, but a final round of 81 put him right out of

'I lost a lot of [US] Opens on greens. I bet I would have won fifteen Opens if I had been a good short putter.'
SAM SNEAD

contention, and in 1947 at the last Snead holed a good putt for a birdie to tie with fellow American Lew Worshan. There was an eighteen-hole play-off, and on the final hole both Snead and Worshan had putts of about two and a half feet to keep them level. Snead thought it was his turn to putt first and settled over the shot. Worshan, perhaps using gamesmanship, raised a doubt and called for the distances to be measured, whereupon it turned out to be Snead's putt after all. He missed, Worshan didn't. Whether they ever spoke again after that incident is not recorded.

Perhaps one of the most extraordinary happenings was his victory in 1946 at the first Open Championship played in Great Britain after the war, the venue St Andrews. Snead wasn't at all interested in playing. He'd entered the

championship in 1937 but only because he was a member of the visiting US Ryder Cup team and they had all agreed to compete. He'd hated Carnoustie and he disliked links golf; in fact, he disliked everything outside the United States. But he had a lucrative contract with the Wilson sporting goods company and its president insisted he play. He said he would only if his great friend and fellow professional Johnny Bulla could keep him company. Now, there's a bone of contention whether this sequence of events is remembered correctly. Some say Johnny Bulla had the opportunity of playing in the British Open, and if *he* could persuade Sam to join *him* it might well endear him to the powers that be and he could end up landing a nice contract with Wilson.

Whatever the truth of the story, they both set off

'I have strong arms and hands from chopping wood. I can still kick the top of the door, and I can stand on the curb and touch the road with my hands.'

SAM SNEAD

for Scotland and after a long sea and train journey Snead looked out to what he described as a raggedy, beat-up old place with something that looked like a fairway running among the weeds. He turned to the other occupants of the compartment and said, 'Say, that looks like an abandoned golf course. What did they call it?' 'St Andrews,' came the reply. Yes, he'd arrived. To Snead it looked like 'the sort of real estate you couldn't give away'. His remarks spread like wildfire; consequently the press did not receive him in a very friendly fashion. He didn't like the hotels or the food, and lived on a diet of baked beans, porridge, strong tea and toast. Times were hard, though; it would be another seven or eight years before the British Isles finally shook off such austerity. At least he thought the caddies would be all right because folklore rated them the world's best. How wrong could they be? Snead wondered. He described the selection before him as a 'bunch of bums' who whistled through their teeth, couldn't put the right club in his hand and smelt strongly of either BO or alcohol, or both.

Thirty-six holes were played on that fateful Friday and there were three players tying for the lead at 215: Snead and Bulla, the inseparable friends, and Welshman Dai Rees. Henry Cotton was a stroke behind with Bobby Locke on 218. Then the wind started rising and so did the scores, everyone dropping shots. Snead took six at the par-four 6th and threw away his club in disgust. He reached the turn in 40 and lost interest in the whole proceedings, but then, bingo!, he birdied the 10th, 12th and 14th, and suddenly he was ahead of the field. From there he coasted home to win by four strokes from, guess who?, Bobby Locke and Johnny Bulla. Perhaps, if Snead had not been coaxed to play in the championship, Bulla would have been the champion.

The first prize was the equivalent of $600 but it had cost Sam $1,000 in expenses to play – not, in

his opinion, the best of business deals. Snead decided there and then he would not come back to defend his Open title, but, unlike Ben Hogan who never did come and play again, he did appear in the 1960s when he was well past his prime, and again for the Centenary Open of 2000. He didn't think much of his 1946 win until much later when the championship became perhaps the most important of all the majors. For years Sam called it 'just another tournament'. He'd hated the cold winds and the bleakness of links golf, uttering the immortal words, 'When you leave the States, you're camping out.' He remained an unenthusiastic traveller, though on many occasions he did venture outside the United States when 'the money was right'.

His putting would desert him, and, unlike Hogan who refused to adopt any sort of putting method other than the one that was supposed to be 'pure', he tried everything to rediscover his form. One-handed, back-handed, croquet style, you name it, Sam tried it, becoming quite proficient at what he called his 'side saddle' style. He did manage to stay free of injury throughout his long career, and his record in tournaments is quite sensational, matched only by Gary Player and Roberto de Vicenzo. When he was 60, Sam finished joint fourth in the US PGA Championship – a remarkable feat. His 81 wins on the US Tour is 11 better than Jack Nicklaus and beats Ben Hogan's record by 19; even such a successful player as Tom Watson is almost 50 victories behind. Amazingly, Sam Snead won over 140 tournaments worldwide. The interesting, dare I say amusing, thing is that total prize money for those 81 wins amounted to $620,126, so you can see why solely to use money won as the criterion for deciding who the best player was is a total nonsense.

Sam Snead – a remarkable talent, and someone who could well qualify as the athlete of the century.

PETER THOMSON

Above **Thomson believed that winning was a product of the mind rather than the swing** (© Empics).

Right **In my book, Peter Thomson is one of golf's supreme champions and life's great companions** (© Empics).

The first time I set eyes on Peter Thomson was on 15 June 1951. I had just that very day completed my stint of National Service in the RAF and had travelled from my father's home near the Ferndown Golf Club into Bournemouth to watch the Penfold Festival of Britain Tournament at the Queens Park Golf Club. So many things were going on in Britain that year, even though austerity still abounded. A hundred years had passed since the Great Exhibition ruled over by Queen Victoria, it was a beautiful day, and there was Thomson holing out on the 18th green – white shoes, dark green trousers, white shirt and tennis visor. Little did I know that that first sighting would lead to a long and dear friendship I like to think has been special to us both.

Right from those early days Thomson had an aura about him, given to few. He simply 'went about his business'. I suppose to some he had an air of superiority which was aided and abetted by this very simplistic approach to the game, but it suited me very well because I had been brought up on such a diet by my father, Percy, who used to say, 'Golf is a difficult game, but we who play it do our best to make it even more difficult.' Thomson found a way to hold the club which was comfortable, albeit with a very strong left hand showing all four knuckles, and he played without a glove, which, if you can do it, is a good thing. At least 95 per cent of professional golfers use a left-hand glove; they feel it gives them a more secure grip, and it certainly helps if the palms get sweaty or you play in hot and exotic climes. Thomson was the first person to have played golf as if it were a game of chess. He was not a long hitter, so placing the ball in the best position for the shot to the green was of paramount importance. If the ground was fast and bouncy he had no hesitation in using a three-wood from the tee, again for position. His game was definitely suited to links golf – the low-flying ball pitching short, running up on to the green, using the contours – and he

possessed one of the coolest golfing brains. These talents made him a superstar.

But for many years there was a 'flaw' in Thomson's record: he achieved little in the United States, winning only one tournament, and that in 1956, the year he won his third consecutive Open Championship. That year he finished among the top ten money winners, and to add to his win in the Texas Open he finished fourth in the US Open behind the winner Dr Cary Middlecoff. His preference for golf in Europe somehow rankled the Americans, who took great delight in pooh-poohing his efforts.

He more than proved them wrong when he reached 50 years of age and tried his hand on the US Senior Tour, which was growing in stature. It only really got going in 1980, and Thomson first made his presence known in 1982, winning just over $30,000. The next year he doubled his winnings, and to the surprise of many was actually practising, seemingly doing his best to return to full competitive sharpness. Things really took a leap forward in 1984 when he won the World Seniors Invitation by one shot from Arnold Palmer – his first victory in the United States for 28 years. He followed that up by winning five of the next nine events, and ended with a tally of nine for the season – quite remarkable, and a record that has not been beaten since. But not for Thomson the continual grind of trying to win ten tournaments every year. He virtually signed off, as if to say, 'There you are, perhaps I didn't beat you twenty years ago, but I'm beating you all today. Goodbye, and thank you for being so generous!'

He's become the elder statesman of Australian golf, captain of the President's Cup team, a rather contrived match between the American Tour and the Rest of the World. He was captain when the event was played in Melbourne a few years ago. His side won, and he uttered the immortal words, 'This is the proudest moment in my golfing life.' I'm

Above **In full swing at the British Open at Royal Lytham & St Annes, 1958** (© Popperfoto).

Right **Putting from off the green at Moor Park, 1962** (© Popperfoto).

sure, knowing Thomson, that was rather tongue in cheek. Surely his victory in the 1965 Open at Royal Birkdale surpassed anything the President's Cup could offer.

At the height of his fame he made very few mistakes, and in his time he has played through a whole tournament without one really poor shot. I don't think there are many who could say that. He rated the avoidance of bad shots more highly than the making of spectacular ones, and I always wonder how he would get on today. I suppose he would be outgunned, but Thomson's greatest weapon was his cool, clinical golfing brain. Like Bobby Jones, Bobby Locke and Walter Hagen, all of them great players, he was not a great believer in long practice sessions. If he was going through a poor patch he would literally sit down, think about it, analyse what he felt was wrong, go to the

practice ground and put those thoughts into practice. After a dozen or so shots, if he was clear in his own mind that he had identified what he was doing wrong, that was good enough. Those thoughts were set in his mind, now there were other things to contemplate.

Thomson believed that winning was a product of the mind rather than the swing, that championships were only partly played on the grass, most of it was decided in the head and the mind was capable of human contrariness (Jack Nicklaus called it course management). He held no affection for the theory that success came from perfection as a result of repetitive practice, honing a swing that hopefully repeated itself under pressure. Once you had learnt how to hit the ball, you had to learn to compete. He could be very philosophical about it. For example, he once came

Why on earth
would a golf
professional want
to read about the
life of Gandhi when
there were Agatha
Christie books
close at hand?

out with the great line, 'Target practice is all well and good, and you might have a badge to say that you arc a truc marksman, but that doesn't necessarily mean you'll be a good guerrilla fighter. You have to have the ability to compete, to survive, not to let the fear of success overwhelm you.'

Thomson was largely self-taught; in his own words, he 'slowly got the hang of it'. Although he was a sociable fellow, in many ways he was a loner preferring to work out his own salvation. I believe he learnt a lot from Bobby Locke – and there were many things to learn, such as the art of pacing yourself around a course and the ability to travel the world with the minimum of fuss and baggage.

He first appeared in the Open Championship in 1951, the only time it was played in Ireland, at the Royal Portrush course, a wonderful venue. He finished sixth. The following year he finished just one stroke behind, beaten by Bobby Locke at Royal Lytham & St Annes. He retained that position when Ben Hogan won at Carnoustie in 1953, but by then it was obvious that Thomson was a special talent and perhaps ready to take centre stage, and in 1954 at Royal Birkdale he did. This time it was Bobby Locke's turn to finish second. This victory marked the beginning of a period of total dominance of the championship at least equal to that of young Tom Morris 90 years before, and one

not bettered even by Tom Watson in the 1970s and 1980s. Indeed, from 1952 to 1958 Peter Thomson finished the Open in either first or second place. When Gary Player won in 1959 Thomson had won three Opens in a row and four in five years, but still the American players and press failed to give him the credit he deserved.

All that changed in 1965. In the field that year were Arnold Palmer, Jack Nicklaus, Doug Sanders, Phil Rogers and Tony Lema. Thomson started with a 74, six strokes behind Tony Lema, and for the first time the spectators saw a new Thomson. He normally smiled and strolled around the course with an easy manner; now he was silent and stern-faced. The final 36 holes were played in a day, and he was paired with Tony Lema, whom he caught after nine holes. The wind was rising, but Thomson went round in 72 in the morning compared to 75 from both Palmer and Lema. A 77 from Nicklaus put him right out of contention. Thomson continued to play steadily in the afternoon, reaching the turn in 34, but then he started to miss a few putts. Nevertheless, he had a one-shot advantage over Lema with two holes left to play, Palmer was on his way to a 79. The last two holes at Royal Birkdale were both over 500 yards, and Thomson needed to finish four, four to be virtually certain of the championship. On both holes he drove straight and true, then threaded long irons between the bunkers to the heart of the green, from there safely two-putting. Meanwhile, Lema finished five, six. Surely this was Thomson's finest hour.

Away from the golf course, Peter enjoyed music, his tastes being quite catholic. He read books that raised an eyebrow or two. Well, why on earth would a golf professional want to read about the life of Gandhi when there were Agatha Christie books close at hand? He dabbled in politics and failed gloriously to win a constituency in Melbourne where his opponent had an advantage of some thousands of votes. His efforts were very creditable, though, and he later served on a nationwide committee looking into the problems of young people and drug-taking. His son, Andrew, went to Japan to study the language and got a law degree. It's hardly any wonder he had a spell in the Australian parliament, and who knows, one day we may see the name of Andrew Thomson followed by the letters 'PM'.

Above **With his second claret jug and runner-up Johnny Fallon, St Andrews, 1955 (© Popperfoto).**

Right **Thomson during his record-breaking round of 63 at the 1958 British Open (© Popperfoto).**

Pages 146 & 147 **British Open, Hoylake, 1956 (© Popperfoto).**

Peter retains his youthful figure, enjoys his wine, loves Australia and is part of a very successful golf course design company, the one responsible for laying out the Dukes Course on the outskirts of St Andrews. It was during this time that he bought a property less than 200 yards from the clubhouse. He spends several weeks a year in late summer at his beloved St Andrews, and regularly walks down to the clubhouse for a couple of scotches before supper. Rather reminiscent of the old days when the townsfolk could see old Tom Morris and the like wandering about the town, very famous yet an integral part of the surroundings. I hardly think

Tiger Woods would be allowed the luxury of wandering unguarded through the streets of St Andrews on his way to an evening aperitif. Perhaps not a scotch, but at least a Coke – Diet, of course!

Despite his 'jolly' exterior, Peter could be very selfish in his relentless desire to be a great player. Perhaps this led to the breakdown of his first marriage to Lois, with whom he had a daughter, Deirdre. He later married Mary and they produced three children, all hale and hearty, and, in turn, their children are proud of Grandpa. And why not, for in my book he's one of golf's supreme champions and life's great companions.

LEE TREVINO

FACT FILE

FULL NAME: Lee Buck Trevino

BORN: 1 December 1939; Dallas, Texas, USA

TOURNAMENT WINS: 73
USA 27
Europe 3
Other 14
US Senior 29

MAJORS: 6
Masters 0 (T10th, 1975; T10th, 1985)
US Open 2 (1968; 1971 after play-off)
The Open 2 (1971; 1972)
US PGA 2 (1974; 1984)
   US Senior Open 2 (1992; 1994)
   PGA Seniors 1 (1990)

US MONEY LIST WINS: 1
1970
   US Senior Tour 2 1990,1992

HIGHEST WORLD RANKING: 21
During 1986 – the first year of ranking

RYDER CUP RECORD:
Appearances & Team Wins (W) 6 (1969–81/5W);
Captain (non-playing) 1985 (0W)
Matches (Won-Lost-Halved) 30 (17–7–6)
Wins (Singles-Foursomes-Fourballs) 17 (6–5–6)

Above **I've marvelled at Lee's lust for knowledge. He'd sit for hours and watch the cricket** (© Popperfoto).

Right **Here was a golfer who could talk, give a stream of quotable material to the press and was able to joke with the galleries in true Bob Hope style** (© Popperfoto).

I have a special place in my heart for Lee Buck Trevino. Why? Because he's a one-off. He came from a most disadvantaged background, never knew his father, and was brought up by his mother Juanita and his grandfather, neither of whom could read or write. His first memories are of living in a four-room shack on the outskirts of Dallas with no electricity, plumbing or windows.

He was about eight when he made his first attempts at the game of golf, knocking pebbles and apples about with an old broomstick. He started helping out at the local driving range, then the owner, Hardy Greenwood, took the boy under his wing and gave him a full set of golf clubs. He oversaw the development of Trevino as a golfer and became the father Trevino never knew. He was entirely self-taught, and when people over the years advised him that his swing was not all it should be, his answer was, 'Show me a teacher who can beat me and I'll listen to what he has to say.'

He left school at the age of fourteen and began to work full time at the driving range before moving on to the local country club. When he was seventeen he joined the Marines where he spent four years, playing quite a bit of golf with officers and their friends. Demobbed in 1960, he became a golf professional and worked as an assistant pro in El Paso, Texas. He was very competitive and loved to gamble. Although they were only small amounts of money, he couldn't afford to lose. When people spoke about pressure in later life, he would say, 'Pressure? These guys don't know what pressure is. Pressure is when you're playing some hard-nosed gamblers for $25 and you've only got $10 in your pocket.' One of his party tricks was to go round the par-three course using a Dr Pepper bottle as a club. I don't know whether any handicaps were involved, but he claims he never lost a match during a three-year period. He played in local competitions and pro ams, had lots of charm and cheek and, even at this very local level, established

a very good rapport with the press and golfing galleries, suddenly finding himself in demand for exhibitions and company days. Lee Trevino was a good golfer, but he also had a ready smile and easy patter.

The year 1965 was the big turning point for Trevino. He did well in local competitions, winning the Texas State Open and coming second in the Mexican Open, and the following year he qualified for the US Open Championship. He played all four rounds, finished just outside the top 50 and went totally unnoticed, but it proved he had a chance, just a chance, of being able to compete at the highest level. Later that year he found himself playing in a couple of money matches in which Ray Floyd was involved, and won them both. His confidence grew, and in 1967 his wife, Claudia, entered him for the US Open Championship which was being played at Baltusrol. Trevino played very well, and with a round to go was just three strokes behind the leader. He closed with a 70, no disgrace for an 'unknown' player, but neither he nor anyone else could match Jack Nicklaus's superb 65. Still, he finished in fifth place and took home a cheque for $6,000, a veritable fortune. This encouraged him to play in more tournaments, and he finished fourth in the Canadian Open. At the advanced age of 28 he was named Rookie of the Year. Just think, he gave Tiger Woods a ten-year start.

Trevino won $26,000 in prize money that year and became a full PGA member. He now knew he could compete with the best, and in 1968 decided to play on the Tour full time. He was still largely unknown to the public and most of his fellow professionals, but this all changed in 1968 when the US Open was played at the Oak Hill Country Club in New York State. The rough was very thick, the greens fast, but these conditions suited Trevino down to the ground. He was a relatively short hitter but he could keep the ball on the fairway.

Above **Awaiting another pay cheque with the help of a beer** (© Popperfoto).

I've invariably found Lee an amazing companion and someone who will always be welcome at my dinner table.

He simply aimed down the left-hand side and cut the ball back on to the short grass. All the trouble on the left-hand side of the course was blocked out, and he went on his merry way opening up with rounds of 69 and 68 to go ahead of the championship favourite, Jack Nicklaus, by five shots. He missed just one fairway in the first round, found the greens with his second shots and holed his fair share of putts.

In the third round he was paired with Bert Yancey, who had a reputation for being a great student of the swing and a lover of the history of the game. He had opened up with rounds of 67 and 68 and led Trevino by a couple of strokes. They were destined to play together for the remainder of the championship. Things went very much Yancey's way in the third, and with ten holes played he was five strokes ahead of Trevino, but then Lee struck with three birdies in the next four holes. Yancey dropped a shot late in the round, and at the end of the day Trevino was just a shot behind. In the press tent afterwards Trevino was a revelation, but for some of the pressmen his attitude was too brash, not to their taste. Surely an 'unknown' could not be so full of confidence, but there he was bragging about his driving and putting and his ability to scramble. If he missed a green he felt sure he could manage to get down in no more than two shots.

On the final day there were just three men in it: Trevino, Yancey, who was leading by one, and Nicklaus, who told his supporters he was going to go for everything, and sure enough he did. He played some wonderful shots but simply couldn't hole the putts, so it became a battle between Yancey and Trevino. For most of the round both were rather poor – they had their moments of brilliance, but there were also a lot of mistimed shots – but Trevino's power of scrambling never manifested itself better than over the closing holes. He fought his way to a winning 69, his fourth round under par, and was for many years the only competitor in the US Open Championship to have played four rounds in under 70. A new personality had burst on to the scene. Here was a golfer who could talk, give a stream of quotable material to the press and was able to joke with the galleries in true Bob Hope style. In fact, some thought he was better than Bob Hope. The money started to roll in. Trevino, very sensibly, stuck to his simple game plan. He did things his way, and in his heart of hearts he felt he could do it again.

However, despite this US Open victory and his good play at various events, some time passed before Trevino was fully established as one of the great players of modern times. His vintage year came in 1971. He won a couple of events on the Tour before arriving at Merion, a beautiful golf course not far from Philadelphia, for the US Open Championship. Merion has a par of 70 and a collection of holes under 400 yards that would bring light to Samson's eyes. Little streams and bunkers, clusters of trees – a veritable jewel. He played quite beautifully and tied with Jack Nicklaus, whom he beat by 68 to 71 in the play-off. Trevino's relatively short but accurate driving proved the key to his victory.

The first tee of the play-off saw some drama, though. Everyone was looking very serious, but Trevino was rummaging around in his golf bag and suddenly pulled out a trick snake which he threw at Nicklaus, who leapt about two feet into the air and was fortunate not to have a thrombosis. The crowd loved it, although I'm not sure Jack appreciated the joke, though, ever gracious, he said to Trevino at the end, 'I'm sure you don't know how good you are. You could win anywhere.'

Trevino went off to Canada and won their Open Championship, then flew to England where Royal

Birkdale was to host the Open Championship. It was Trevino's third attempt, and his first round was typical of his scrambling. He missed four fairways and both the short holes but was still out in 33 having had only eleven putts. He finished with a 69 and was at the top of the leaderboard with three other players, one of whom was Tony Jacklin, at that time at the height of his powers. The next day both he and Jacklin scored 70, Trevino's putter once again proving to be a magic wand. The crowd were definitely on Jacklin's side and this rankled Trevino for a spell. His good shots were greeted with polite clapping whereas whatever Jacklin did was received with rapturous applause. Nevertheless, he went round in 69, one shot ahead of Jacklin and Mr Lu. Who will ever forget Liang Huan Lu, the smiling Formosan who captivated everyone with his neat golf, impeccable manners and the way he raised his hat to all and sundry at least 50 times a round?

Trevino's outward nine in the fourth round was quite amazing. He single-putted seven of the first eight greens to be out in 31. He had a four-stroke lead with nine holes to play – the championship was all but sewn up. He remarked later, 'I was having so much fun I almost forgot to finish the tournament.' Lack of concentration certainly caught up with him on the 17th. Instead of the usual fade, Trevino hit it high into the sand hills on the left and found an awful lie. He took a great slash at the ball but moved it only a yard or so. Still in loose sand, he then managed to get the ball out, but only across the fairway and into the rough on the other side, eventually ending up with a seven.

Below **Chipping in on his way to securing the British Open title at Muirfield, 1972 (© Popperfoto).**

Not many players over the years have won the championship with such a score on their card, Bobby Jones at Hoylake in 1930, Peter Thomson in 1955 and Bill Rogers in 1981 the notable exceptions. With his lead reduced to just one things were tight, but a par at the final hole was good enough. He'd won three national Open Championships in little more than a month.

He loved links golf, enjoying the bump-and-run shots, entirely different from those required at the Augusta National – or so he thought. I think this negative thinking was one of the reasons he never figured prominently at the Masters, although a number of players far less skilful than he walked away with the green jacket.

Trevino returned in 1972 to defend his Open title. He was brimming with confidence and he loved the venue, Muirfield, the home of the Honourable Company of Edinburgh Golfers, some twenty miles to the east of Edinburgh. But there were other players whose confidence was also at a high level. Nicklaus, for example, was on the crest of a wave. He was the holder of the US PGA Championship from the previous year and in 1972 had won both the Masters and the US Open. Could he win all four majors consecutively, a feat

never achieved and only approached by Ben Hogan in 1953?

Many words have been written about the Open Championship of 1972. Although there have been many great occasions when extraordinary feats of skill and derring-do have prevailed at this great event, 1972 would be hard to beat for the sheer number of 'happenings' that went on. Jacklin was playing superb golf; Nicklaus, who appeared out of touch with the leaders, was six strokes behind with a round to go; Trevino was playing like a man inspired, hitting the ball straight and true, holing out from the most unlikely places. It didn't seem to matter whether it was from grass or sand, Trevino's ball went unerringly towards or right into the hole.

How well I remember that final day. Nicklaus, who had been so far behind, reached the turn in 32 and then birdied the 10th and 11th. Eleven holes played, just 38 strokes taken, and at this point he led the championship. He played the rest of the round well, though there were no more birdies – in fact he'd dropped a shot at the par-three 16th – and was round in 66 to set a very good target. Trevino and Jacklin were going at it in ding-dong fashion, two heavyweights trading punch for punch, but at the 17th it looked all over for

Right **Looking to hole out on Troon's 7th green, 1989** (© Popperfoto).

Below **Playing out of the rough at the Piccadilly World Matchplay Championship, 1972** (© Empics).

One of his party tricks was to go round the par-three course using a Dr Pepper bottle as a club.

Trevino. He found a bunker on the left from the tee, played out and was still well short of the green in three in thickish rough, but he just walked in and smashed at the ball, which ran several yards through the green up a little bank. At last it was Jacklin's turn. He was just short of the green in two and played a reasonable pitch to within fifteen or sixteen feet. He'd got there in three, Trevino was over the back of the green in four.

There have been many interpretations of how quickly Trevino struck his fifth shot. In fact, having seen the pictures many times, I think he took a little longer than many people supposed. The ball landed on the green and ran straight into the hole for a par five. Trevino jumped up and down like some wild dervish; Tony Jacklin's face, on the other hand, betrayed no emotion. He had a go at his birdie putt and went perhaps a yard past. Then he missed the return and Trevino was overjoyed. Jacklin dropped another stroke at the final hole to finish third behind Jack Nicklaus.

Trevino played the hole quite beautifully and won his fourth major championship. It wasn't his last, either. In 1984 he won the US PGA Championship at Shoal Creek in Alabama.

What a glorious period it had been, though. In the early 1970s for four years Trevino was never out of the top four on the US money list. But he suffered from back problems, and an operation he had in 1976 didn't seem to do him an awful lot of good. Furthermore, his choice of management team was disastrous. The money had flowed in over the years but, owing to some catastrophic business moves, it disappeared much quicker. Trevino never complained, he just set about making another fortune. Still, for a number of years his business acumen was not the greatest and neither was that of those he entrusted with his fortune. I always remember, after his second financial fiasco and on one of his many trips to our Pro-Celebrity Golf series at which he was such a welcome guest, he remarked to me that we were

Trevino married for the third time in 1983 – coincidentally, to a second Claudia. He said it worked out very well because he didn't have to change the initials on the bathroom towels!

Above **His second claret jug, 1972 (© Popperfoto).**

Right **Contemplating matters at the 1991 British Open (© Empics).**

Pages 156 & 157 **Lining up a putt before an intrigued gallery, Wentworth, October 1973 (© Empics).**

both lucky in being able to earn money so easily with our various skills. I was flattered that he'd bracketed me with him, for certainly his golfing skills far outweighed mine.

Trevino married for the third time in 1983 – coincidentally, to a second Claudia. He said it worked out very well because he didn't have to change the initials on the bathroom towels! She came out with an equally good saying. When he was complaining that he was too old to be in the business, she remarked that his golf clubs had no idea how old he was so he should get out there and start performing. Sure enough, he did: he turned 50, joined the Senior ranks and was immediately successful, building yet another fortune, which hopefully remains intact. From his three marriages he has had four children. Perhaps the last ones have been the luckiest for he has made more time for them, whereas before he put golf well ahead of the family, but I believe that motivation was to escape from his early life of poverty.

For my money he's one of the best companions, although I'm not sure many other golf professionals would say that. For them, too much Trevino can be a pain in the neck! I've marvelled at his lust for knowledge. Whenever he came over to Britain, particularly when we had our Pro-Celebrity week, which was always recorded in August, he'd sit for hours and watch the cricket. He'd ask me about the rules and how it was played, and although I'm no expert, I passed on what knowledge I could, not only about cricket but about local government, how England, Ireland, Scotland and Wales were all different and had their own characteristics, how parliament was run, the roles of kings and queens and the royal family. He read and enjoyed British newspapers, not just the ones with the naked ladies but ones that actually had stories to tell and articles you could learn from.

Lee Trevino, an unorthodox giant in the game of golf. It will be a long time before we see his like again.

TOM WATSON

FACT FILE

FULL NAME: Thomas Sturges Watson

BORN: 4 September 1949;
Kansas City, Missouri, USA

TOURNAMENT WINS: 51
USA 34
Europe 5
Other 8
US Senior 4

MAJORS: 8
Masters 2 (1977; 1981)
US Open 1 (1982)
The Open 5 (1975 after play-off;
1977; 1980; 1982; 1983)
US PGA 0 (T2nd 1978)
  PGA Seniors 1 (2001)

US MONEY LIST WINS: 5
1977; 1978; 1979; 1980; 1984
  US Senior Tour 0
  Highest: 13th 2001

HIGHEST WORLD RANKING: 4
During 1986 – the first year of ranking

RYDER CUP RECORD:
Appearances & Team Wins (W) 4 (1977–89/3W)
Matches (Won-Lost-Halved) 15 (10–4–1)
Wins (Singles-Foursomes-Fourballs) 10 (2–4–4)

Above **British Open winner, Troon, 1982** (© Phil Sheldon).

Right **Watson at the 2000 US PGA Championship, Valhalla Golf Club, Louisville, Kentucky. He finished a very creditable equal ninth** (© Phil Sheldon).

Watson was rather a slow starter. Relatively early in his career he had a chance to win tournaments, and indeed a major or two, but when in sight of the winning post he stumbled. Many thought him a 'show pony' – all frills and flounces and no substance. How wrong they were. Watson had what many would call a 'good brain' and gave, and still does to this day on occasion, the impression of being a 'superior being'.

About 5ft 9in and nicely proportioned, he never set out to be a fashion plate. His hair was long and unruly, his trousers always looked as if they belonged to somebody else – a bit long, or a tad short – and his shirts were either tight and skimpy or gaping at the neck. Many times he insisted upon wearing a tweed cap, particularly when golfing in Britain; most of the time it didn't fit, so it didn't do him any favours. He looked at his best in a tennis visor, at his worst in a jockey cap. Having said that, once Tom got the idea of how to win he was on his way, although some of his early traits certainly remained.

He was a stickler for the rules and was not afraid of confrontation, challenging a number of the top players when he felt they had perpetrated a misdemeanour. He was also a beautiful striker of the ball, with a full swing which went just past the horizontal in the backswing and a full follow-through, a fine player with the long irons and, for a period, a master putter, particularly within a range of ten feet in.

It was 1975 when he made his first appearance in Britain for the Open. Up to that time he'd won only two other events, so surely his prospects were not very strong, yet very quickly he became a British Open specialist. He just kept going, hitting the fairways, hitting the greens, sneaking a putt here, getting down in two from a bunker there – all those were his early trademarks. There were a number of contenders on that last day in 1975, some of them very well known, others about to

make their mark: Johnny Miller, Jack Nicklaus, England's Neil Coles, Bobby Cole from South Africa, of whom much was expected, and a youthful, flamboyant Australian by the name of Jack Newton. Many might have thought they had an opportunity of winning that championship, but the end result was a play-off between Watson and Newton. Newton had certainly had opportunities to win it in normal time, but perhaps the one player who had had the best chance of all was Bobby Cole, but at the end of the four days' play a par at the last hole was good enough for Watson.

It was the start of a wonderful run. Every time Watson came to play in our championship he looked a likely winner, and for a period he virtually dominated events in the USA too. In some ways I think Watson was surprised by his 1975 victory. Two years later, in 1977 at Turnberry, he appeared to me to be a much more rounded player, exuding confidence and striking the ball with ridiculous ease. The course was firm and fast, and he and Nicklaus dominated the event. Like two heavyweights they went at it blow for blow, having their own private game while the rest of the exalted field competed for third place.

The duel between these two, particularly the final two rounds, was one of the most intriguing it has ever been my pleasure to see – drama right to the end. On the penultimate hole Nicklaus missed a five-footer to give his rival a lead of one, Watson's honour. The tee shot struck the middle of the 18th fairway, which that year was being played as a dog-leg right to left; Nicklaus's reply zoomed away to the right and was rather fortunate to stop just short of thick gorse bushes. From there he smashed it as hard as he could and just got on to the front quarter of the green. Watson struck a short iron right at the flag, down it came and ended, oh, less than a yard from the hole. The crowd were ecstatic, surely it was all over. But no,

'When I was a student at Stanford I would play Pebble Beach, and I had these dreams. I'd be playing the US Open and come to the last three holes saying if I par them I win against Jack Nicklaus – and that dream came true.' TOM WATSON

'Not as good as a few, but better than most. Let's just put it that way.' TOM WATSON ON HIS PLACE IN GOLF HISTORY

Left **Working on the putting line during the 1997 Masters – the year Tiger Woods won by twelve strokes (© Phil Sheldon).**

Right **Watson won the second of his five British Opens at Turnberry in 1977 (© Phil Sheldon).**

there was still more drama to come. Nicklaus prowled around and eventually settled over the putt and struck it beautifully. Somehow one sensed it might go in – no, surely it couldn't? – but it did. The crowd by this time were salivating. Watson stepped up, took little time over the putt, and struck it firmly into the hole. It went in at great speed and for a split second I thought it might spin out, but no, it was there, they'd halved the last hole in three, Watson the champion by one. I shall never forget the scenes as those two walked off the green, arms around each other's shoulders, the end of an amazing championship. At the prizegiving the American golfer Hubert Green, who finished third, remarked, 'Well, I won the tournament I was playing in.'

Watson continued to play his own game. Not for him rushing off to some golfing guru with declarations that he was going to learn to play the ball left to right or right to left, to hit it higher or lower, or to be more consistent, he just got on with it. Helped by Byron Nelson at times, Watson had a very firm grip, he was brisk and breezy, and although the occasional drive would wander off line, he was the complete article.

Despite all the success he continued to live in American's Mid-West, with his wife, Linda, one of his biggest supporters and loudest critics. To most of the outside world their marriage appeared to be secure, but then, after many years, it came to a very acrimonious end.

Two shots of Watson's stand out in my memory. Firstly, his second shot to the Road Hole in the 1984 Open Championship at St Andrews. He certainly overclubbed, but he struck the shot as purely as it was possible to do. The ball landed on the green, which was firm, went through and clattered into the famous wall. He managed to scuttle the ball back on to the green, but he took five and lost the championship. Seve Ballesteros, holing a good putt on the last, was the champion. Watson's routine was pretty much the same for every shot he played, but perhaps that second shot was played rather hastily. The only thing wrong with it was it went 25 yards too far.

Secondly, his amazing chip-in at the penultimate hole at Pebble Beach in the US Open Championship of 1982. His great rival Nicklaus had completed his final round and Watson needed a par, par finish to tie. Now, the 17th at Pebble Beach is a short hole that has been lengthened over the years and was, I'm sure, never designed to receive a two- or a three-iron – that's the club that has to be played when into the wind. He struck his tee shot well but it bounced left and went into thick rough some three or four paces off the edge of the green. Watson then employed his brisk method of chipping, a style I'd seen dozens of times from close quarters when he had come over to participate in our BBC Pro Celebrity Golf series from the Gleneagles and Turnberry Hotels. One, two, three, pop, up it went, and when the ball was easing its way towards the hole Watson started running on to the edge of the green pointing at the hole with his club. In it went – a remarkable shot. Now, of course, he only required a par at the last to win. In fact, he got a four to win his first US Open Championship by two shots.

There was a story that did the rounds that Watson was approached by a television company and asked whether he would re-enact that shot – rather reminscent of Jean van der Velde being asked to retrace his momentous steps down the 18th hole at Carnoustie when his chances of

Above **Lifting the Ryder Cup at the Belfry, September 1993** (© Empics).

Above right **Weighing up a putt before clinching the fourth of his five claret jugs, 1982** (© Popperfoto).

Pages 164 & 165 **Trotting over a bridge at Turnberry during 1994's British Open** (© Popperfoto).

winning the 1999 Open Championship disappeared in a flurry of ridiculous mistakes. Watson refused. Why? Well, perhaps he didn't want to put his skills to the test. There is another version of the story: Tom went back many times, though of course the rough is never always quite the same, and tried the shot time and time again, never getting it any closer to the hole than several feet away.

The golden years of Watson were undoubtedly from 1975 to the mid-1980s, during which time he took over from Jack Nicklaus as the world's leading player. He was the leading money winner in the United States four years in a row. He'd won the Masters a couple of times, and he'd won our Open Championship five times in the space of nine years. It was perhaps during his period of coming over to play in the Pro Celebrity Golf and the various Open Championships, in which he was so successful in Scotland, that Tom got a flavour for whisky – not that it ever really took a big hold on him, but he did enjoy a taste come the end of play. Many times we had a 'toddy for the body'.

As the years ticked by his magical putting stroke began to fail. Though the style looked exactly the same, firm and decisive, something was wrong and he started to miss. He turned 50 and joined the Senior ranks, and although he has been successful he has won nowhere near as many times as many of us thought he would. Perhaps the desire to win is diminishing a little.

Watson has a definite love of the game and often takes time off to play 'friendly' golf in Ireland and Scotland (on many occasions carrying his own clubs), two of his favourite venues being Ballybunion on the west coast of Ireland and Royal Dornoch in the far north of Scotland. He was always very much his own man and appeared not to have many friends within the profession. He had majored in psychology at Stamford University, but the degree was for Business Psychology, whatever that may mean. At the time of writing he still lives in the Mid-West enjoying, he says, the occasional touch of bad weather. He's even been known to go out with red golf balls in the snow.

Tom Watson, a giant of the game. With that permanent half smile playing round his lips and the tousled hair, he really does look like and live up to his nickname, Huckleberry Finn.

TIGER WOODS

FACT FILE

FULL NAME: Eldrick Tiger Woods

BORN: 30 December 1975;
Cypress, California, USA

TOURNAMENT WINS: 47
USA 36 (37 with co-sanctioned Open
Championship, 2000)
Europe 4
Other 7

MAJORS: 8 (11)
Masters 3 (1997; 2001; 2002)
US Open 2 (2000; 2002)
The Open 1 (2000)
US PGA 2 (1999; 2000 after play-off)
US Amateur 3 (1994; 1995; 1996)

US MONEY LIST WINS: 5
1997; 1999; 2000; 2001; 2002

HIGHEST WORLD RANKING: 1
7 times (total 261 weeks,
the last 191 consecutive) 1997-13 May 2003

WALKER CUP RECORD:
Appearances & Team Wins (W) 1 (1995/0W)
Matches (Won-Lost-Halved) 4 (2–2–0)
Wins (Singles-Foursomes) 2 (1–1)

RYDER CUP RECORD:
Appearances & Team Wins (W) 3 (1997-2002/1W)
Matches (Won-Lost-Halved) 15 (5-8-2)
Wins (Singles-Foursomes-Fourballs) 5 (1-2-2)

Above **Tiger is a truly remarkable
talent whose name will forever be
in the record books** (© Popperfoto).

Right **Limbering up before the
Canadian Open** (© Popperfoto).

When Jack Nicklaus burst on to the golfing scene many people were open-mouthed. Here, surely, was the ultimate golfing machine, and his remarkable career stretching over 40 years didn't disappoint us. People involved in the game of golf had been familiar with the name Eldrick Woods for many years. He first appeared in public on a televised Bob Hope show. There he was, aged about two, coming on to the set with his father and hitting a couple of plastic balls into the audience. A new golfing messiah, they said. Heads nodded, but many wondered at what age this boy's love of golf would disappear.

As it turned out, it didn't, and he went from strength to strength, putting incredible scores together while still a child. Before he left his teens he had won the Amateur Championship of the United States three years in a row. On a couple of occasions he was dead and gone with a few holes left to play but was able to produce golfing miracles to see him through to victory. He was getting to be one of the most famous sporting figures in America. He secured a place at Stanford University and told all and sundry that he would definitely complete his studies before considering taking up golf professionally. Again, things didn't quite work out that way, and for whatever reason (goodness knows it couldn't have been for money!), midway through the 1996 season he joined the professional ranks. If he could win enough money in the handful of tournaments left before the season's end, he wouldn't have to go through the stresses and strains of the qualifying school, which borders on the Spanish Inquisition. He qualified for the final 36 holes every time, won a total of $760,000, and finished 24th on the money list – a sensational start to a career.

His father pontificated long and hard, a strange man who had seen service as an officer in the Green Berets, a US regiment of great renown rather like our own Royal Marines or SAS. Some of his utterances were outrageous. His son was going to be more famous than anyone the world had ever seen. He was going to do more good than Gandhi, Mother Teresa, the Pope and Tony Blair all rolled into one.

It was getting to the end of the 1990s when Tiger played in his first Masters as a professional. Many, including me, thought, 'Well, now we'll see how he gets on when he's out with the big boys in this cauldron of excitement.' In the first round he took 40 for the first nine. Words like 'I told you so' were bandied about, but then he roared home in 30 for a very respectable 70. He went on to pulverise the field and win by a distance. By this time the father had changed his son's name by deed poll from Eldrick to Tiger, a name with a certain ring to it, and why not? He was certainly baring his teeth to the golfing world.

For a period Tiger seemed to win where and when he liked, able to produce the most amazing shots when most needed. Millions of dollars rolled into his coffers, and everywhere he went he was surrounded by security. How long could this young man in his early twenties stand being under such scrutiny? Strangely enough he seemed to relish all the adoration, even though he must have found it difficult to enjoy a 'normal' lifestyle. He moved from California to Florida, where the tax laws are far more helpful and to be near a number of his golfing friends. He was fast acquiring the trappings of wealth, flying by private jet when competing in world events. It was said he was being paid up to $2 million just to compete.

Then his father suffered a heart attack, and for some months it looked as if he might not survive. But he did, and, thankfully, he has taken a back seat over the last year or so. Tiger's mother, on the other hand, seems to be there when needed, and I'm sure it's her brand of Far Eastern positive thinking, spiritualism, mental control, call it what you will, that has been such a tremendous help to

'I won twelve times around the world in 2000, including three majors, and I remember hitting only one shot I would call perfect – a three-wood on the 14th at St Andrews in the third round of the British Open.' TIGER WOODS

'The best year of my life was when I was eleven. I won 32 tournaments that year. Everything's been downhill since.' TIGER WOODS

Above **Another expertly executed bunker shot** (© Popperfoto).

Right **Tiger prowling Augusta's 12th fairway** (© Popperfoto).

Tiger. She has a certain serenity about her, and although that would perhaps be the wrong word to use as far as Tiger is concerned – particularly when you see him mouthing obscenities at the top of his voice or smashing a club into the ground – he still has the power to recover, to withdraw inside himself and in a few seconds regain his composure. Whether this is the case, or it's just a good bit of acting, I don't know, but he is able to produce many magical moments when needed.

He's about 6ft 2in tall, weighs about twelve stones, hits the ball miles and appears to have every part of the game under control. At the outset of his professional career he wasn't slow to show arrogance bordering on rudeness, but then, in the space of a few months, a transformation took place. I didn't think it was possible for anyone to learn so much about 'things', not just about hitting a golf ball but about playing the 'game of life' and giving 'them' what they're looking for. It requires a ready smile, a cheery word, signing just enough autographs, going unforced into the press room,

and just being available. It's all done with style by Tiger, although I'm sure under his breath he's murmured a few obscenities to help him through those stressful moments when the press are snapping at your heels, all of them trying to get that extra snippet of information that'll catch the headlines the next day. I'm told he regularly gets death threats, which can't be the most relaxing thing in the world. He's having to contend with jealousy, envy and racial intolerance too, a myriad of things that seem to plague society more these days than years ago.

Early in the new century Tiger was going through what for him is a slight lull. People have wondered, 'Did it all really happen? Did he really win those four championships in the space of twelve months, or was it all a dream?' No, it was real enough, and he's still only in his mid-twenties. As if to confound the doubters, he turned on some magical form over the last nine holes of the Williams Challenge played at the dramatic Sherwood Oaks Golf Club near Los Angeles in

Left **Extricating himself from St Andrews' rough, July 2000** (© Popperfoto).

Right **The frustration of a missed eagle putt** (© Popperfoto).

'Golf to me isn't just something to do. I love this game.
It's like a drug I have to have.' TIGER WOODS

Pages 172 & 173 **Receiving Augusta's traditional green jacket from Vijay Singh** (© Popperfoto).

mid-December 2001. A handful of strokes behind Vijay Singh with nine holes to play, he suddenly took off with four (or was it five?) birdies in a row. A slight dip from Vijay, and Woods had won. First prize $1 million, immediately donated to his Foundation.

Where will the road lead? Who knows? I do know it's been a privilege to see him play, but perhaps it's too early to say he is the greatest player of all time. People were saying things like that back in the 1890s about the Morris family, but he's certainly the most dominant player in the world of golf at this time, and one who has learnt to put on an air of graciousness, even if a much harder personality lies just beneath the skin. But he's doing the right things most of the time and people

are on his side, they're willing him to win. What a wonderful asset that is whenever you walk out on to the 1st tee, to feel the warmth of the crowd welling up around you, wishing you well, instead of an oppressive silence and mumbled remarks suggesting rather grudgingly that they admire your play but they don't like you. Any hint of that happening to Tiger Woods was dispelled early on, and for that he must take a great share of the credit, as must his family and those one or two close friends and advisers who have whispered sound words in his ear which Tiger has been able to take on board and use to his advantage.

He is a truly remarkable talent whose name will forever be in the record books. If he could only learn not to spit on the course, he'd be perfect!

WOMEN IN GOLF

It's a matter of record that Mary Queen of Scots was out playing golf on the Musselburgh links when her husband, Lord Darnley, was being put to death. So you can see, women have been around the game for many years, though how on earth they managed to swing the club wearing skirts that reached the ground and bodices so tight they could hardly breathe is beyond me. They were definitely second-rate citizens until well into the twentieth century, but since then they've made huge strides.

The earliest and most famous woman golfer was unquestionably **Joyce Wethered**. Born in 1901, she almost made it to the end of the century before she finally went to the great country club in the sky. She was simply remarkable. The great Bobby Jones said she was the best player, man or woman, he had ever seen – perhaps an exaggeration, but who's to argue? Henry Cotton was also of the opinion that she drove the ball as far as a good club player, and her use of pitching clubs, her chipping and putting were all accurate and precise, but it was her overall straightness which made her such a formidable figure.

She didn't come from a wealthy family, and of course the thought of a woman turning professional in those far-off days was absolutely taboo. How different it could have been for her had she started out on her career today. It's remarkable when you consider she played 38 matches in the British Ladies Championship and won 36 of them, winning the championship in 1922, 1924, 1925 and 1929.

Then, suddenly, she gave up championship golf and mainly played in mixed foursomes events around London and the Home Counties. She married Sir John Heathcoat-Amory and lived a genteel life, spending her latter years in the magnificent Knightshayes House some ten miles or so from Tiverton in Devon.

Above **Joyce Wethered at Portrush, October 1920** (© Empics).

Left **The flamboyant and demonstrative Mildred Didrikson on Wentworth's East Course, July 1951** (© Popperfoto).

It was the Americans, as usual, who really got the ball rolling when they created the American Ladies Professional Tour just after the Second World War, and how lucky they were to have the three best women players in the world all turning professional at the same time: Babe Zaharias, Louise Suggs and Patty Berg. What a trio! Although things didn't immediately flow like milk and honey, it wasn't long before they were well and truly on their way.

Mildred Didrikson – a familiar name? Well, perhaps not, but she was a key figure in the evolution of women's golf. She was one of the great athletes in the 1932 Los Angeles Olympic Games where she won the javelin and the 80 metres hurdles. Then, having set the world record in the high jump, she was disqualified for using the western roll – considered, would you believe, to be unladylike! She could do just about everything. She was an all-American basketball player, and just before the Olympics entered eight events in the US National Championships, winning six of them and setting four world records. It was like a decathlon, only worse, as all these achievements were crowded into just two and a half hours – yes, two and a half hours. What a woman!

She came from a poor background, and the only way it appeared she would make any money was through sport. It was a difficult time for most people, but particularly so for a woman from the wrong side of the sticks trying to make a living in sport – so many rules, regulations, pitfalls, hang-ups and taboos – but the moment she got her hands on a golf club she immediately saw golf as a way of making progress. She went from strength to strength, hitting the ball miles. The only trouble was she was treated as something of a freak on exhibition tours. For a while it was just a question of how far she could hit the ball – shades of Sam Snead, perhaps – but she learnt quickly. Joyce

Wethered was one player who showed her there was a lot more to golf than just hitting the ball a long way. The amazing thing was her ability to adapt and learn, and so quickly. She soon realised there were many more things to learn about the game of golf compared to running, hurdling and throwing the javelin.

But the world continued to be against her: she was barred from playing in amateur tournaments because she had played other games professionally (that certainly wouldn't be a problem today). However, round about this time she met and married the famous wrestler George Zaharias. After a short while Mildred Didrikson suddenly emerged like a butterfly from a chrysalis with a new name, 'The Babe', which then became Babe Zaharias, and that was the beginning of a truly remarkable set of events.

She recovered her amateur status in 1943 and, in 1946 and 1947, won seventeen consecutive tournaments, rivalling the achievements of Byron Nelson. The most important was the US Amateur Championship, a matchplay tournament; Babe won the final eleven up with nine to play. She then went on to become the first American to win our Ladies Open Championship. She had to play six rounds and, would you believe it, she lost only four holes during all that time.

But now the LPGA had been formed and she was ready to go professional. In her short eight-year career she won 31 of the scheduled 128 events. In 1950 she won six out of nine, and seven out of the fourteen played the following year. By this time another player, Betsy Rawls, had joined the scene and was providing some very strong opposition. Babe visited Britain again with the US women's team to play a match against a team of first-class London amateurs. She was drawn against Leonard Crawley, a former English champion, and beat him quite comprehensively, having rejected his offer for her to play off the forward tees. In 1953 it was discovered she had cancer, and she underwent a series of major operations, but she came back the next year to win five more events, including the US Open by twelve shots.

The cancer, though, was well ensconced in her body, and despite another series of operations in the mid-1950s she passed away in 1956 at the young age of 42. She died an icon. How I wish I had seen her play when in her prime.

Below **Mildred Didrikson with the British Open trophy aboard the liner *Queen Elizabeth* on her return to the US, June 1947 (© Popperfoto).**

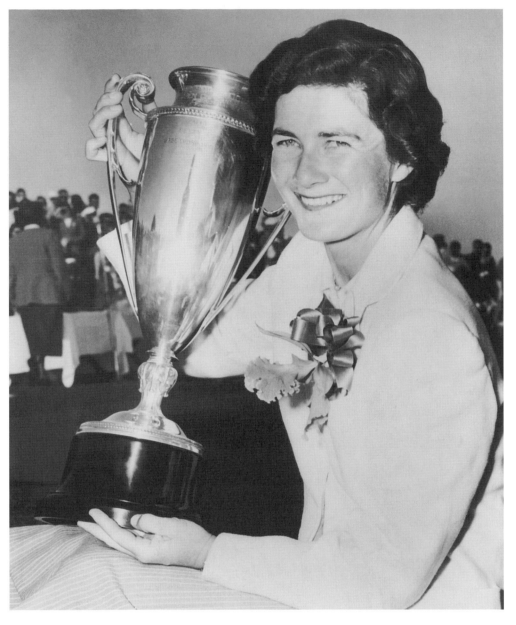

Louise Suggs was not a big woman and relied on rhythm, balance and timing to get length, which she achieved in the most brilliant fashion.

Louise Suggs was one of the most elegant women players the world of golf has ever seen. Born in Atlanta, Georgia in 1923, her career lasted from the late 1940s to the early 1960s. She was not a big woman and relied on rhythm, balance and timing to get length, which she achieved in the most brilliant fashion. She was soon winning tournaments and championships by enormous margins. For example, in the 1950 US Open she won by fourteen shots. She became the first member of the LPGA Hall of Fame, which may seem a little strange because she had won only four professional golf tournaments, so the decision to place her in the Hall of Fame must have been based primarily on her achievements while an amateur. In 1952 she won six events, eight the following year. She was a leading money winner in 1953 and pretty much always finished near the top of the tree, though sadly a lot of the records are incomplete, as many things were 50, 60, 70 years ago before the days of computers and microchips. Her last win came in 1962. Altogether she won 50 times on the LPGA Tour, a total beaten only by Kathy Whitworth, Mickey Wright and Betsy Rawls. A remarkable woman, and one of the most beautiful of golf players.

Above **Patty Berg** splits yet another fairway, August 1963 (© Empics).

Right **Mickey Wright** may well be the greatest female golfer the world has ever seen (© Phil Sheldon).

Patty Berg was born in Minneapolis, Minnesota in 1918. One of the founders of the US Ladies Professional Golf Tour, Berg was a rare talent. The first signs were displayed in 1935 when she faced Glenna Collett-Vare in the final of the US Ladies Championship. Collett-Vare was the greatest player in the 1920s and early 1930s, and this was to be her last appearance in a final. For Patty Berg, aged seventeen, it was her first. On this occasion experience triumphed over youth, Collett-Vare winning by 3 & 2, and in 1937 Berg again reached the final and lost, this time by 7 & 6 to Estelle Page. However, the following year everything in the garden was rosy when she met the same opponent in the final, this time coming out on top by 6 & 5. Although she was only 20 she was nearing the end of a very successful amateur career during which she had won 29 titles and 40 important tournaments in all, and been part of the US Curtis Cup team in 1936 and 1938.

In 1940 she signed professional forms with the sporting goods manufacturers Wilson. There was no tour as such for women then, so her role was to play exhibition matches and give demonstrations while furthering the cause of the mighty Wilson company. This she did to tremendous effect. In fact, Wilson was one of the earliest companies to see the full value of having professionals, both men and women, using its equipment, making sure its goods were seen worldwide. One of the reasons for their high profile was the very distinctive red and white golf bags their contracted players carried, with the player's name written in script down the white side panels of each bag – every bag the same, yet different.

In 1942 Patty sustained a severe injury, the first of many misfortunes and spells of ill health. Her knee was smashed in an accident, and it was set so badly that the bones had to be rebroken and reset three more times before they eventually healed. In 1943 she won a couple of minor events before doing war service in the Women's Marine Corps, then in 1946 she stepped out with her fellow professionals into an entirely new career. Between 1948 and 1962 she won 42 events, and in the 1950s she was declared the player of the decade, always winning at least a few events each year (her top tallies were seven in 1953, six in 1955 and five in 1957). She was leading money winner in 1954, 1956 and 1957, and won the Vare Trophy, the ladies' equivalent of the Harry Vardon Trophy, for the lowest stroke average for the year in 1953, 1955 and 1956. In 1952 she set a record which stood for more than twelve years with her round of 64 in a tournament in Richmond, California.

In the latter years of her life she underwent operations for cancer and also had major hip surgery. Patty Berg won most of the awards on offer in golf and was one of the most active people in promoting the game, teaching children and working for cancer research, a true, well-rounded professional with a heart of gold who enhanced the lives of those with whom she came into contact.

Mickey Wright, born in 1935 in the fair city of San Diego, had a short amateur career, playing only one full year of amateur golf in 1954 during which she won the world and all-American titles, though she was beaten in the final of the US Ladies Amateur. She turned professional in 1955, and by 1958 was the Tour's leading player. Between 1961 and 1964 she won 44 tournaments, setting all sorts of records along the way, notably thirteen victories in a season, closely followed by eleven wins in another calendar year. By 1964 Wright was averaging just over 72 strokes per round in competitive play, a remarkable level of consistency. Kathy Whitworth holds the record for career wins with 88 tournament victories, but Mickey Wright won her 81 in a much shorter time, between 1956 and 1969.

For some reason round about the mid-1970s she lost some of her interest in the game and went back to college, though she suffered from an arthritic wrist, reacted badly to the sun (not something with which an outdoor person wants to contend), had a fear of flying and had problems with her feet. That's why she played most of her competitive golf wearing what in those days were called plimsolls, nothing like the sturdy trainers or tennis shoes available today – another reason why she had to learn to swing with rhythm.

She was a very quiet person, not at all like the flamboyant character of, say, Babe Zaharias. She really did let her clubs do the talking. She much preferred to be out of the public eye, and golf writers soon learnt to concentrate on the way she played, not on what she said. Her swing was thought of as perfect, and very few, if any, approached her crisp action when hitting the long irons. Although Mickey was a relatively low-profile legend, mainly because of her natural shyness, she may well be the greatest female golfer the world has ever seen. Certainly for a period she was the most dominant player in the history of women's professional golf. In later years Judy Rankin, who became one of America's finest women professional players, remarked that 'Mickey Wright's golf made the golfing world sit up and take notice, and when they started looking past her they saw us, and we went from strength to strength thanks to her and her amazing skills.'

'I would have swapped being the first to make a million for winning the [US] Open.'
KATHY WHITWORTH

Kathy Whitworth was born in 1939 in Monahans, Texas, and whenever her name is mentioned you automatically think of a parallel career. Whose? Sam Snead's. Although both of them were prolific winners of tournaments, Whitworth bagging a remarkable 88 of them, neither won their respective US Open titles. Between 1965 and 1973 she was the leading money winner every year except one. Although total career earnings of a million dollars have now become commonplace, Kathy Whitworth was the very first person to get to that figure, in 1981.

When she turned professional in 1958 she had a couple of state titles to her credit, but no one could have foreseen that she would go on to such great heights. But she did, soon challenging Mickey Wright for the position of the most successful woman player ever. She won eight events in 1963 and repeated the feat in 1965, but even more successful seasons lay ahead: 1966 (nine titles) and 1968 (ten). But more and more women were coming into the game, standards were getting higher and higher, and she was getting older. Her victories became less frequent, though she won at least once every year up until 1978.

Her main strength was her ability to keep the ball in play. She had a workmanlike swing but was an exceptional putter. Her whole life revolved around the game of golf. Sadly, some financial investments didn't work out for her, and instead of having a bed of roses and a life of smoked salmon and caviar, Kathy has to settle for a more modest lifestyle. A remarkable talent.

Left **A deft touch from Kathy Whitworth at Mission Hills, 1984** (© Phil Sheldon).

Jo Anne Carner smoked as dramatically and as stylishly as Ingrid Bergman or Dean Martin.

Jo Anne Carner, née Gunderson, was another woman I enjoyed watching, not only because of her skill, but also her tremendous personality. Born in 1939 in Kirkland, Washington, Jo Anne had the most amazing career as an amateur, winning the US Championship five times before deciding to turn pro at the age of 30. At the age of 18 she became the youngest amateur champion since the late 1900s. Her amateur record is staggering, and she was the darling of the United States Golf Association.

She was known as the 'Great Gundy', and although not by any stretch of the imagination a pretty woman, she had a presence that was, to my way of thinking, completely overwhelming. She had a wonderfully slow, hippy, rhythmical walk. She smoked, but she didn't just smoke, she smoked as dramatically and as stylishly as Ingrid Bergman or Dean Martin. She liked a glass of beer, too, and had a wonderfully open face framed by short, fair, curly hair, a broad mouth, strong teeth and a ready smile, the look of someone you could completely trust in whatever situation you found yourself in.

She had a victory in her first year as a professional and won the Rookie of the Year award, finishing eleventh on the money list, which was worth a touch over $14,000. The following year, however, she won the Open Championship, which made her the only woman ever to take both amateur and professional titles, plus the US Junior Championship. By 1975 she was well established as one of the greatest of professional players, and from then until 1984 ninth on the money list was her worst year, having been in the top three on seven occasions and having topped the table in 1972, 1982 and 1983.

By this time she was in her mid-40s, and the Great Gundy had become Big Momma. She had also become the all-time leading money winner. During her career she banked more than $2 million, some £1.7 million more than Ben Hogan did during his playing days. That's why, as I've said elsewhere in these chapters, trying to equate people's skills with the amount of money they've earned during their career is an absolute waste of time.

Just a couple of years short of her fiftieth birthday she tied for the US Open Championship and lost in a play-off which featured Laura Davies, and a year later she was twenty-first on the money list, even though her appearances were becoming fewer and fewer. She was a wonderful long-iron player, hitting the ball as well as many male professionals. During her career she won 42 LPGA events, and though she only plays for fun now, she has enhanced the world of golf with her robust earthiness and the fact that she's just 'a damned nice person'.

This book is all about people in the world of golf I've admired or been intrigued by, and **Catherine Lacoste**, born in Paris in 1945, is certainly one of those. She went into semi-retirement in her mid-20s, but in the space of a few years had left her mark in the history books of golf, having won, as an amateur, the British Ladies Championship in 1969, the US Women's Open Championship (against all the pros) in 1967 and the US Women's Amateur in 1969.

Catherine came from a very famous sporting family. Her father, René, was one of the three musketeers of French tennis in the 1920s and 1930s, for it was he, Henri Cochet and Jean Borotra who achieved so much for themselves and their country on the world's tennis courts. Among other things, and with a little bit of help from his friends, he had created the famous Lacoste sports shirt (you know, the one with the crocodile on the breast pocket). Her mother was France's best female golfer in the 1930s.

Catherine was just a few days past her twenty-second birthday when she won that US Open Championship in 1967, and when you look at the array of professional talent lined up against her, her achievement is simply mind-boggling. She shot a second round of 70 and took a five-stroke lead, which she later increased. With victory in sight during the final round a few errors began to creep in, but she didn't fail, despite having to face a very partisan American crowd. At the end of the day she won by two, at that time the first to win the championship as an amateur, the youngest player ever to win, and only the second overseas player to do so. Then, dammit, just two years later she had an even more outstanding year, becoming only the third woman to win the British and US amateur titles in the same year.

It was then that she got married, became Madame de Prado and tiptoed into semi-retirement. She did, however, play in the Spanish Amateur in 1972 and 1976, and, of course, won them both! Oh, and by the way, she also managed to win the French Ladies Open four times. She was a powerful hitter and a master with the short irons. She was sparky, cheery, talented and, although she came from one of France's most famous sporting families, she was determined not to be known as the daughter of the Lacostes. She made her own shadow.

Catherine came out of the Lacostes' collective shadow and made a considerably larger one for herself, and it couldn't have happened to a nicer person.

Above **Reaching for an iron. Nancy Lopez at the US LPGA Championship, 1981** (© Phil Sheldon).

Left **Catherine Lacoste was sparky, cheery and talented** (© Popperfoto).

Nancy Lopez was born in the small town of Torrance, California in 1957. She had a first-class amateur career which earned her team places in the Curtis Cup side and World Team Championships, but somehow the US Women's Amateur Championship eluded her. It was obvious to anyone with half an eye that, although she had rather a slow, plodding swing, she had rhythm, balance, timing, and kept the ball pretty straight – and when she got within sight of the flag she was deadly.

She turned professional in 1977 when she was just 20 and found success immediately with a second-place finish. In 1978 she was still classed as a rookie but she went on to set all kinds of records, winning nine tournaments in all. So, not only did she end up being named Rookie of the Year, she was the leading money winner, Player of the Year and the Vare Trophy winner with a scoring average of 71.76. Five victories in a row brought a sudden resurgence to the fortunes of the LPGA Tour, and literally thousands more spectators turned out to follow this charming girl of Mexican extraction.

She was once more the leading money winner in 1979 with another eight tournament wins. At one point during those first two years she had won 17 events out of a total of 50 entries.

Obviously her success rate had to slow down a little bit because, as happened with Tiger Woods, the other players on the circuit suddenly thought they'd better buck their ideas up if they were going to give Miss Lopez a run for her money. Nancy continued on her merry way, now winning two or three times a year, which was looked upon as almost mundane. But she had married and become a mum, so her values had changed. Still, in 1985 she won five tournaments including the LPGA Championship, and pocketed more than $400,000, setting yet another record. Once again she was voted Player of the Year and won the Vare Trophy for the third time, her scoring average improving all the while as that year it was 70.73. She notched up 21 top-ten finishes in her 25 appearances, which showed an outstanding degree of consistency, but her run of twelve consecutive top-five finishes was even more impressive.

Nancy had a wonderful smile and an outgoing personality, all very appealing. She now had two daughters to look after, but still she enjoyed her golf and made a very lucrative living. But it wasn't all plain sailing. Her rather laborious, nay laboured backswing sometimes took the club face to a very shut position at the top of the swing. This meant that if her timing was a little bit out she could hook the ball violently, but she always had her excellent putting stroke to fall back on.

Before long she'd won her thirty-fifth career tournament and been entered into the LPGA Hall of Fame, only the eleventh player at that time to qualify. By the end of 1988 she had raised that tally to 39 and had won over 2\frac{1}{4}$ million. Surprisingly, she had yet to win the US Women's Open, and in fact at that time had only two major championship wins on her record.

She continued to play through a few marital problems, but she was very much a homemaker. Now in her early 40s, she is one of the game's icons. Those of us who saw her play in her prime have only fond memories. A charming, attractive, smiling, dark-haired young girl with time for everyone, making the game look fun. I wish there were a few more like her around today.

During the final round of the 1996 Evian Masters, Laura carried a portable television in her bag to watch England's football match against Spain. She won the tournament by four strokes.

Laura Davies, born in Coventry in 1963, is one of the dominant figures in the modern world of ladies golf. Laura had a relatively short career as an amateur but she won several important events and played in the Curtis Cup matches of 1984. It was in 1985 she decided to turn professional, and was immediately successful, topping the money list in her first two seasons.

The main strength of her game is her enormous length and powers of recovery, although at times she has a rather wayward and inconsistent putting stroke. She took herself off to the United States and did quite well in her first US Women's Open, finishing eleventh, and when she played in the 1987 US Open Championship it was only her fourth time playing on the US Tour, although she had caused a few ripples earlier in the year when at the Dinah Shore Tournament, played at the delightful Mission Hills Club in Palm Springs, she opened with a round of 66. Sadly she didn't continue in that happy vein, and eventually finished well down the field in thirty-third position. There were no such mistakes at the Plainview Golf Club in New Jersey, though, and she won with rounds of 72, 70, 72 and 71. This is the event that Jo Anne Carner, 'Big Momma', should have won, but she made rather a mess of the final hole, resulting in a three-way play-off which Davies won.

Laura was becoming something of a phenomenon. Her drives were averaging 255 yards, against that of 220 for the rest of the field, and on one occasion on a hole measuring almost 500 yards she became the only woman ever to have reached the green in two. Her career at the very top of the tree is perhaps beginning to draw to an end with the emergence of so many new young players, particularly from the Far East, but Davies will be remembered as a great supporter of women's golf around the world and I like to think she's had fun along the way. Golf has not been the totally dominant thing in her life, though. She likes to gamble, and some over the years have been slightly worried about what appears to be careless abandonment when finding herself near a casino or race track, but she says she has it under control. Whether that's true or she's in denial only she knows. She has a delightful home in Surrey, enjoys playing other games and loves fast cars. British golf has been enhanced by her presence and playing skills.

Above **Annika Sörenstam drives at the 9th hole during the Du Maurier Classic in Quebec, August 2000 (© Popperfoto).**

Left **Laura Davies assesses a putt during the 1996 Wilkinson Sword English Open (© Empics).**

climatic conditions, and although there are many first-class courses in the country there are also a large number that have somehow just 'happened', rather like some of those in Japan, created on very difficult terrain: temporary tees perched high up in craggy rocks, narrow fairways, a short season, lots of indoor driving ranges. You wonder where on earth they managed to acquire their skills. But they have and we should be grateful.

But **Annika Sörenstam** is a remarkable talent. I hesitate to use the word 'veteran', but she seems to have been around a long time now, and apart from a couple of short spells has always been right at the top of the tree. Her play, particularly towards the end of the 1990s and the start of the new century, was quite dazzling. Not only has she made herself a huge fortune (which I hope is managed well), she has managed to do it with a minimum of fuss, though some people seem to think that because she doesn't skip, jump, swear, spit, wear outrageous clothes or go round with a permanent smile on her face she hasn't 'given enough back to the game'. A female Lee Trevino she certainly is not, but she has a style of play that's most interesting. On pretty well every shot her head seems to be up well before the club head has struck the ball, yet there's hardly a finer striker of the ball in the world of women's golf. She went through a period of feuding with her sister, Charlotta, but they now seem to be back on track, although Annika is the much better player.

There is surely still a number of good years left in Annika, who continues to set golfing records. One of the latest was a round completed in 59 shots on a 'proper golf course'. Sweden should be very proud of its golfers, both male and female, and perhaps more than anything they should be proud that the system which was set up gave young people an opportunity to play at the highest level, and ordinary folk with no aspirations of becoming champions the opportunity to enjoy the game of golf.

When the Ladies' European Professional Golf Tour began I was privileged to be asked to be its first president. I thought they were on an absolute winner. There were some very attractive players around and surely sponsors would jump on to the bandwagon in an effort to advertise their wares through women's golf? But it didn't work out that way as pretty much all the good continental players beat a path to the United States.

One country to provide a whole gaggle of first-class women players was Sweden. Now, why on earth should that be? – well, your guess is as good as mine. They're certainly not blessed with the best

Karrie Webb from Australia was, for a period, the most dominant player in women's golf. She had a swing in some ways rather similar to Annika Sörenstam's, though in the on-course smiling stakes Annika is a Jim Carrey compared to Webb. But being an extrovert on the golf course without the ability to match does not pay the bills. Webb has certainly achieved some miraculous scores over the past few years and went through a couple of seasons when she appeared invincible.

'In my view, she is the best golfer, male or female, there is. She has a better swing than Tiger Woods.'
PETER THOMSON ON
KARRIE WEBB

'Golf is a game where there is always room for improvement. You can never master it.'
KARRIE WEBB

Above **Annika Sörenstam and Laura Davies** sign autographs at the 2000 Women's World Cup tournament in Kuala Lumpur in Malaysia. Go and watch women's golf, learn and enjoy (© Popperfoto).

Left **Karrie Webb** chips on to the green at the McDonalds LPGA Championship at the DuPont Country Club in Wilmington, Delaware, June 2001 (© Popperfoto).

Some pundits think the American Women's Tour is going through a rather dull period at the moment because on so many occasions it is virtually a two-horse race between Webb and Sörenstam, although Korea's Se Ri Pak and one or two others from the Far East have entered the arena and given things a touch of spice. I don't really know what people want. I presume that in an ideal world they'd like about twenty attractive women with wondrous swings going at it ding-dong week in, week out, the opportunity of seeing a great cross-section of brilliant play and a different winner coming up every time. There have been occasions in history when that has occurred, but at this moment it's fair to say there are no more than ten players who appear to have that magical quality which stirs the sporting blood and drags spectators through the turnstiles.

We marvel at modern players, but it was the same, to a certain degree, back in the days of Joyce Wethered, Jean Donald, Wanda Morgan, Patty Berg *et al.* Of course there was no television then and the only way things were kept for posterity was if the event was grand enough to merit the

attention of either Pathe or Movietone News. It really was a question of being there and seeing it happen. Perhaps that's where the old joke began: 'I bent down to pick up my programme, looked up and it was all over.'

The Women's Tour in the United States was rather badly affected for a number of years by the growth of the Men's Senior Tour. At the moment, just because they're a little bit becalmed, people are quick to say they don't have the 'characters' of yesteryear, but there are plenty on the horizon and the Tour is already roaring back to steal some of that television viewing public who enjoy watching women's golf.

A tip to ponder. Most male golfers would learn a lot from watching women's golf rather than men's. Why? Because they have to 'punch their weight', use balance, rhythm, timing. You might pick up a tip watching Tiger Woods when he plays a bunker shot or a little chip from the side of the green, but there's no way you're ever going to hit the ball like him. So wherever you are and whenever you get the opportunity, go and watch the women, learn and enjoy.

GOLF'S INFLUENTIAL PEOPLE

Apart from the great champions who have been mentioned in this book, it would be wrong of me not to include a number of people and organisations who have contributed to, and enhanced, the world of golf in various ways. Some may be unfamiliar to you, others well known, but in my opinion they have all been enormously important in the progression of the game.

On the administrative side, **Gerald Micklem**, a lifelong amateur member of Sunningdale, Captain of the R&A and on virtually every committee devised by man, a lover of golf and one of great foresight. **Keith McKenzie**, largely responsible for the resurgence of our Open Championship while Secretary of the Royal & Ancient Golf Club. An ex-Gurkha officer, he was flamboyant and forthright, someone ideally suited to that particular time. **John Jacobs**, golf pro, master teacher and one of the few people who helped sculpt the PGA European Tour as we know it today. **Ken Schofield**, the secretary of that association who in his own way has worked wonders for European professional golf and has seen the Tour grow to its present proportions. **Sir Michael Bonallack**, one of our greatest amateur players who for a number of years was Secretary of the R&A. Michael went about his work in an entirely different way to Keith McKenzie but was hugely respected by all who had dealings with him.

Joe Dey, not quite Bonallack's American counterpart but nonetheless an exalted figure in the United States Golf Association and a huge contributor to the game and its forward thinking. **Frank Hannigan**, for a number of years the chief executive of the USGA. He brought about many changes to the internal regime of that association and pushed through the seemingly impossible task of seeing the US Open Championship played on one of their few links courses, Shinnecock Hills in New York State. 'Too small a site, no way in, no way out,' they said. 'It'll be an absolute disaster.' But it wasn't, and crusty old Hannigan was vindicated. **Sandy Tatum**, the original Yank at Oxford who played in the university team just after the war, a respected San Franciscan lawyer who held pretty much every position on the various USGA committees.

The contributions of the **Royal & Ancient Golf Club of St Andrews** and the **USGA** in general have made the game what it is today, and they have always done their best to retain its integrity.

Mark McCormack, the founder of IMG, whose influence one way or another has affected so many facets not only of golf but other sports and, in some cases, life in general. **Binnie Clark**, in the mid-1960s the events manager of Gallagher, the giant tobacco company among whose products were Senior Service cigarettes, who for a time ran a superb golf tournament. Clark was the first man to introduce a tented village, proper toilet facilities and somewhere to leave your left luggage. We can't thank him enough for his foresight.

From the world of television, CBS's **Frank Chirkinian**, who, despite some shortcomings, brought many innovative ideas to golf coverage in the United States. The same can be said for **Terry Jastrow**, husband of actress Ann Archer, an energetic young producer/director who has one of the most fertile minds I have ever encountered and who has been associated with some great television successes, including the resurrection of *Shell's Wonderful World of Golf, The Three Tour Challenge* and many other TV specials. The innovative **BBC Sports Department**, particularly when it was under the guidance of **Jonathan Martin**, envied throughout the length and breadth of the world for the quality of service. **Australian Television Sport** has also introduced many superb innovations into a number of sports.

And what of the writers who have given us so much pleasure? **Pat Ward Thomas** of the *Guardian*. **Henry Longhurst**, who for 25 years never missed his article for the *Sunday Times*, for his BBC coverage on radio and in the early days of TV. **Peter Ryde** of *The Times*, **Herb Warren-Wind**, one of the most revered American journalists, **Leonard Crawley**, for many years the golf correspondent for the *Daily Telegraph*, a beautiful golfer and cricketer of the highest level who was part of the MCC team which toured the West Indies in 1925/26, **Ian Wooldridge** of the *Daily Mail* and **Norman Mair**, whose wife, Lewine, now writes for the *Daily Telegraph*. How I wish he had been employed by them, for no one can wax lyrical or tell a golfing tale better than Norman.

Karsten Solheim for his innovative ideas on golf club design, followed closely by **Ely Callaway**, who said his success was all down to 'marketing, smoke and mirrors' (he was being too modest). **Club Car**, **Yamaha** and **Eezee Go**, three golf cart manufacturers whose products play such a big role in so many areas of life. **Footjoy** and **Titleist**, two manufacturers who have turned out 100% quality products since day one. The early club makers at St Andrews who burnt the midnight oil in their quest to produce clubs for the players of the day with quite meagre tools. The early sporting goods companies: **True Temper, Slazenger, Dunlop, Ben Sayers, Wilson, Spalding, McGregor** *et al*. And the caddies, from the earliest days to today's stars, now so much an integral part of the game, particularly **Jimi Cousins**, who worked with me so successfully

through the 1960s and is sadly no longer with us.

Jesse Valentine, **Jean Donald** and **Wanda Morgan**, three of the first women professionals in the UK. **Lady Angela (Ward) Bonallack**, one of Britain's top lady amateurs and charity workers, and someone who is such fun to be with.

And the great amateurs whose feats sometimes go unnoticed as things were quite different way back then. Many remained lifelong amateurs and gave the likes of me enormous pleasure as I followed their various sojourns into the world of international golf year after year. Irishman **Jimmy Bruen**, who at the age of sixteen was favourite to win the Open Championship at St Andrews in 1939, and **Joe Carr**, a wonderful swashbuckling golfer – how lucky Ireland was to have two such wonderful ambassadors. **Ronnie White**, an Englishman, member of the Royal Liverpool Golf Club, perhaps better known as Hoylake, the most professional-looking amateur I have ever seen. **Peter McEvoy**, who not only won the Amateur Championship twice but went on to become a superb leader of men. How did he do it? I'm not sure, but his inspirational captaincy of the Walker Cup sides in the latter part of the twentieth century was amazing. **Deane Beman**, who couldn't hit the ball out of his own shadow but had the most wondrous short game any human being has a right to be blessed with. He had a wonderful amateur career in the United States, made a bit of a showing as a pro, then took over the reigns of the United States Professional Tour. Under his guidance, it grew to gigantic proportions. **Gary Wolstenholme**, my godson, Britain's top amateur and co-host (with me) of the Grand Match, played each year at the Royal Cinque Ports Golf Club. What fun – old Ryder Cuppers v. Walker Cuppers.

Golf club secretaries who played a part in my life and added to my 'view of things' are quite numerous, but at the end of the day four stick firmly in my mind. **J. C. Beard**, for many years secretary at the Ferndown Golf Club when I was a youngster. A portly, ruddy-faced man who had a couple of daughters who were very fine golfers, winning the Ladies Dorset Championship on numerous occasions and bringing a touch of glamour to the proceedings. Beard was a very progressive man and a keen student in the study of pesticides, weed killers, etc. but also mindful of the need to preserve the flora and fauna. **J. D. 'Daddy'**

Bond, the secretary at Parkstone Golf Club, where my brother Alec and I spent thirteen very happy years. He had a wonderful solution for members' problems: if anyone complained he'd listen attentively, then say, 'I understand your point exactly. If you'd like to let me have it in writing, I'll put your complaint before the committee and it will be dealt with.' The aggrieved member went home, poured himself a cup of tea or a large whisky, whatever was his wont, then totally forgot about it. The letter was never sent and the flesh wound healed in a very short time. 'Daddy' should have been in politics.

The other two were both secretaries at the Honourable Company of Edinburgh Golfers, better known as Muirfield, some twenty-odd miles to the east of Edinburgh, two extraordinary characters. **Colonel B. Evans-Lombe OBE** and **Captain P. W. T. 'Paddy' Hanmer RN retd**, each, in his own way, unique.

Evans-Lombe goes back a long way, the first secretary I ever met who was truly eccentric. He used to arrive on a huge bicycle, a cross between an early Raleigh and a Penny Farthing, around his neck a huge pair of binoculars taken from a U-boat commander. One of his great tricks when a visitor came to play was to look across the course, raise the binoculars and say, 'Well no, I don't think so, we're very busy today, but give it an hour then you can start off the 10th – but just nine holes!' The visitor hoping for a round would look out and, if he were in luck and had twenty-twenty vision, espy in the far distance two members and a labrador.

Evans-Lombe was one of the first secretaries to build up this mystique of formidableness, but Hanmer carried through in fine style, although unfortunately he could be rude on occasion. I was fortunate enough to get on with him, but some of his remarks to visitors were mind-boggling. For a long period it seemed as if the committee and members were not all that bothered; all they wanted was a financially sound club, stunning weekend lunches, a continuous supply of kümmel and port, a welcoming in-house staff, and greenkeepers who cared for the links. So long as those things were in place, their last concern was for the well-being of visitors – unless they were their own guests!

There's one great Hanmer story. After Tom Watson won the Open at Muirfield in 1980, Hanmer repaired to a local hotel to have dinner. It was still daylight when someone rushed in and said, 'Captain Hanmer, Captain Hanmer, there are people playing on the golf course!' The gallant captain left the table, went up to the club, and there, coming down the final hole (so it's reported), was Tom Watson and (perhaps) Ben Crenshaw, fuelled by a little alcohol (some versions even have their wives teetering along beside them in their three-inch heels). They had played up the 10th and down the 18th using hickory-shafted clubs and gutty balls – great fun.

Hanmer was incandescent with rage. He rushed on to the green shouting, 'What do you think you're doing? *Whatever* do you think you're doing? Who are you?'

To which Watson supposedly replied, 'Paddy, you know who I am, I've just won the Open Championship.'

'I don't care about that!' Hanmer retorted. 'What the hell are you doing out here playing on the course? It's closed! Be in my office in the morning at nine o'clock!'

'But, Paddy,' Watson reasoned, 'we're going back to America tomorrow, we're leaving at—'

'I don't care about that!' Hanmer spluttered. 'You be in my office tomorrow morning!'

The rest of the exchange has rather been lost to the passage of time, but it is believed they repaired to the clubhouse, had a few after-dinner drinks and everything quietened down.

Of course, Muirfield and other great clubs are in a unique position. Many people want to come and play and, sadly, don't always go through the right channels, which can create problems. But the fearsome reputation of previous secretaries remains. Many try to copy their moods and methods, but at the end of the day only a few are one-offs. Beware if you happen to be on the wrong end of that sort of barbed tongue. Life can be interesting and, on occasion, painful.

And what of the **greenkeepers**? How well I remember the groundstaff arriving at Ferndown on their bicycles when I was but a lad. Now things are much more sophisticated and there are machines to do most of the work. But my hat always comes off to those greenkeepers who stayed at a golf club long-term, who knew the ground and when to do what to it, sometimes thwarted by greens committees who knew absolutely nothing about the subject, eventually, through their meddling, having to move on. And what of all the wondrous tools that have been invented for them over the years by Torro, Jacobson and the rest, although sometimes I think they helped to take away the ability of greenkeepers to use their legs.

That's just a small sample of those I've been fortunate enough to meet along the way. There are hundreds more, wonderful fellow pros and people of my youth and beyond such as the Whitcombes, Christy O'Connor, Ken McIntyre, Hugh Lewis, Arthur Lees, Dai Rees, Max Faulkner, Harry Bradshaw, Fred Daly, Jimmy Adams, Ken Bousfield, Eric Brown, Charlie Ward, David Thomas, Ray Floyd, Fuzzy Zoeller, Hale Irwin, Payne Stewart, Sandy Lyle, Jimmy Demaret, Tommy Bolt, Roberto de Vicenzo, Phil Mickelson, Kel Nagle, Clive Clark, Jeanne Bisgood and Maureen Garrett.

And, finally, **John Martin** and **Joe Catford**, who between them invented, devised and marketed the PowaKaddy, the world's most successful powered trolley for the golfing public, still the best in the business after so many years – and what a joy if looked after properly!

PETER ALLISS WOULD LIKE TO THANK:
• Robinson Holloway for her statistical contribution to this book.

THE PUBLISHERS WOULD LIKE TO THANK:
• Alun Evans, author of *The Golf Majors: Records & Yearbook* series
  (2002 edition published by A & C Black), for providing the statistical data for the Fact Files.
• Everyone at Smith & Gilmour.
• Jen Little at Empics.
• Ian Blackwell and Andrew Wrighting at Popperfoto.
• Rick Mayston at Allsport.
• Gill and Phil Sheldon.
• Daniel Balado.